LINUX FOR NEWBIES

become an Open-Source computer hero

Marek Mularczyk

www.SaiTraining.co.uk

Linux for Newbies - become an Open-Source computer hero

Published by Sai Training

ISBN - 978-0-9571214-2-3 (Paperback)
ISBN - 978-0-9571214-3-0 (PDF)

www.saitraining.co.uk
www.marekmularczyk.com

For my beloved daughter Julia
who passed away as I started writing this book

and for my beloved wife Monika
who always believed in me.

Table of Contents

5 Get up to speed with Linux 65

6 Get productive with Linux 95

7 Working with graphics 121

8 Multimedia 165

9 Beyond Basics 181

Introduction

Welcome to this book. This book will guide you through the world of Linux and I am going to show you how to install one of the most popular distributions of Linux – Kubuntu. This book will cover Kubuntu version 11.04.

I will try to challenge you here, because you're going to discover some new things here, you will discover how the open-source software opens new possibilities and how it is developed. First of all, you need to change the way you look at the software, Linux opens new possibilities as a free operating system, free to download, free to install, and you feel free to sell it if you want.

I know it's hard to understand at the beginning especially as you probably have been using proprietary (not free) operating systems for some time (you probably are a Windows or Mac user). What most people don't know is that when you purchase a proprietary software, you are not really the owner of the software, you are given a license to use it. That's it. Linux also has a license, but it's different from proprietary software. Linux is distributed under the GNU General Public license (GPL), which basically means that the software is open to use and modify by anyone, and I mean really anyone.

There are a number of different Linux distributions. Let me give you a quick overview of the most popular ones:

Ubuntu/Kubuntu

Quite a new, but at the same time powerful distribution. It quickly became one of the most popular Linux distributions (according to many sources it is the most popular Linux distribution at the moment – as of December 2011). The release cycle is six months for distribution updates and a number of applications that can be installed from their repositories is impressive.

Open SUSE

Another distribution which have received very positive feedback from the community. It has easy to use configuration tools, YAST, with many packages available. I have used Open SuSe in the past and I was very happy with it. Like most other Linux distributions it includes both Gnome and KDE desktop environments. Open Suse is being developed in Germany.

Mandriva

Mandriva, formerly known as Mandrake, is being developed in France. It became very popular as an easy Linux distribution near the end of the twentieth century. It is based on Red Hat distribution. It is known for its simplicity of use and for an easy to use installer.

Now, a few words about Kubuntu.

Kubuntu has a brother called Ubuntu. They are both developed by
the same vendor. The major difference between Ubuntu and Kubuntu
is that they come with different graphical environments: Ubuntu
with Gnome and Kubuntu with KDE. Both distributions are being
released at the same time, so if you decide that you want Ubuntu with
Gnome, you can also download and install version 11.04.

Kubuntu/Ubuntu come from one of the best and oldest Linux distributions – Debian. If
you have never heard about Kubuntu or Debian, that's ok. Most people haven't. Debian
is perceived as one of the most secure and stable Linux distributions. Because Kubuntu
comes from Debian, all Debian software will run on it, so you can choose from thousands
of free applications! Some reasons why I use Kubuntu (I have used many different Linux
distributions in the past) are because it is easy to install and use, easy to install additional
software and it is a powerful operating system. If you haven't used Linux before, do not worry.
You will find Linux easy to get used to. Just have a look at this screenshot of my desktop.

Do you notice some familiar applications? Of course you do! There is Firefox on the right (although if you prefer you could easily install Chrome) and Thunderbird to the left – an email client that works on Windows as well. In the top left corner you can see Gimp – a graphics editor, kind of like Photoshop for free. Again, Gimp runs on Windows as well so you may have used it in the past.

Also notice how clean, tidy and easy to understand the Linux environment is. There is a main menu button in the top left corner (like the Windows logo on Windows). Because I'm using Kubuntu which is KDE based, you can see the KDE logo (you will find it on every Linux distribution that runs on KDE). That's where the main menu appears as you can see below:

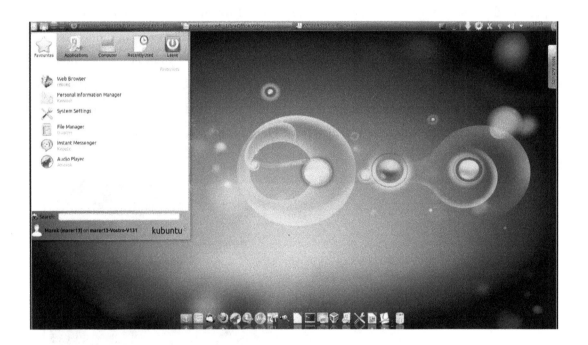

Oh, and by the way, did I mention that with Linux you can install loads of software straight from within your operating system? No?

No more searching through the internet trying to install Skype or MPlayer or Firefox etc. That's how you do it on Windows, that's not how we do it on Linux! You'll absolutely love it! Also, in case you have never used Linux before, many applications you have used before run on Linux.

Just to name a few:

- Firefox,

- Thunderbird,

- Skype,

- Libre Office or Open Office,

- Adobe Reader etc.

If the application you're using on Windows or Mac doesn't run on Linux, most probably there is an alternative application on Linux, i.e. Libre Office or Open Office are fantastic replacements for Microsoft Office.

This book gives you all you need to get a quick start in using Linux to get it up and running really quickly. And remember that because Linux is open-source, feel free to make as many copies of your Linux distribution as you want. Nobody is going to sue you.

To install Kubuntu you will need to download it and burn it onto a cd.

You can download Kubuntu 11.04 from the link below:

Kubuntu 11.04 (Intel x86) download – for almost all PCs.

Kubuntu 11.04 (AMD64) download – 64bit machines.

If you are not sure which one to download, download the first one. It will run on all Intel machines (including Mac systems) and all Windows machines.

1 Why Linux and a Brief history of Linux

Welcome to Linux – an amazing free open-source operating system with a number of free applications.

Let's start with some history to give you some background about Linux and how it all started.

The history of Linux begins back in 1991, when Linus Torvalds, a student at the University of Helsinki at that time, came up with an idea for a new operating system that would suit him better than Windows. He wanted to create a new operating system that would be based on UNIX. Unix is a powerful operating system that was developed back in the 70s, but it had one disadvantage – it was expensive (nowadays it is not just Linux that is based on Unix, but also Mac OS). So Linus decided to create his own operating system based on Unix and that's how Linux was born!

The Linux logo you can see here on the right is a penguin called Tux - created by Larry Ewing in 1996 after being suggested by Alan Cox and refined by Linus Torvalds.

The first official version of Linux appeared in 1994 (Linux 1.0). One of the fantastic features of Linux back then (and still nowadays) was that it ran smoothly on the less powerful computers, it didn't have (and it still doesn't) such high demands to run it like other operating systems. It could easily run on a 386 processor with less than 2MB of RAM.

One of the fantastic decisions that Linus made was to release Linux as a free operating system, so anyone could install it for free and distribute it or even change it. This with time brought a number of different Linux distributions. Nowadays there are hundreds of various Linux distributions. Linus made it clear at the beginning that Linux has to be free, not proprietary. He made it Open Source. This is something amazing about Linux. Everyone can change it, create their own Linux distributions and distribute them.

Because Linux became an Open Source software, not proprietary, this started a quiet revolution. People started contributing to Linux and it lead to improvements and innovations. That's how Linux became popular.

Let me give you one example of the improvements in Linux and one of my favourite features. When using Linux, you can work with a number of virtual desktops, so you could seperate your work – you can work in a web browser on one desktop, work with Libre Office on another desktop, and so on. Basically, you can work on many desktops without all the clutter you got on other operating systems like Windows or Mac OS. And to make it more interesting, Linux has had this feature for many years! I still haven't seen anything like it on Windows.

Because Linux is Open Source, it is open to changes and improvements unlike proprietary operating systems like Windows or Mac OS. With the proprietary operating systems, only a selected group of people knows the insides of the system and only they can make any changes, improvements to it. Proprietary systems are a bit like a closed, sealed box.

At the time when Linux was born, there were two major operating systems, two major competitors – Windows and Mac. On PCs it was actually just Windows as Macs were very expensive (they still are). At that time, consumers couldn't afford Macs so Windows sneaked into every corner of the world. But this starting slowly to change at the beginning of the 90s with the release of Linux.

In August 1991, Linus posted a famous post about the birth of Linux, that became famous all over the internet. Here is just a part of it, the most famous one perhaps:

```
I'm doing a (free) operating system (just a hobby, won't be big and

professional like gnu) for 386(486) AT clones.
```

What Linus didn't realise back then was that he was going to change the computing world forever. Soon after the release of Linux hundreds and later Welcome to Linux – an amazing free open-source operating system with a number of free applications. Let's start with some history to give you some background about Linux and how it all started.

The history of Linux begins back in 1991, when Linus Torvalds, a student at the University of Helsinki at that time, came up with an idea for a new operating system that would suit him better than Windows. He wanted to create a new operating system that would be based on UNIX. Unix is a powerful operating system that was developed back in the 70s, but it had one disadvantage – it was expensive (nowadays it is not just Linux that is based on Unix, but also Mac OS). So Linus decided to create his own operating system based on Unix and that's how Linux was born!

The first official version of Linux appeared in 1994 (Linux 1.0). One of the fantastic features of Linux back then (and still nowadays) was that it ran smoothly on the less powerful computers, it didn't have (and it still doesn't) such high demands to run it like other operating systems. It could easily run on a 386 processor with less than 2MB of RAM. Thousands of people joined the project to start improving Linux. Soon many commercial vendors joined creating their own versions of Linux, including additional software and bundling it together. That is also how Kubuntu was created that I am going to use here to guide you through the 'Linux world'.

On the page here you can find a diagram with the major Linux releases (kernel versions) from the beginning to present day (source: Wikipedia):

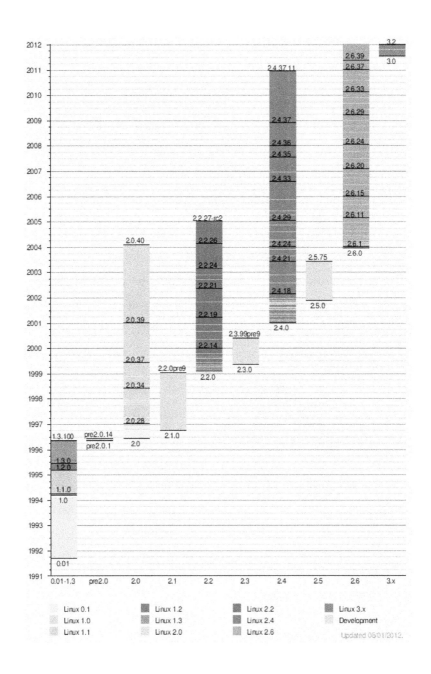

What's great about Linux is that it runs on so many different platforms. It runs not only on PCs, but also on Macs and mobile devices (the most popular Linux on mobile devices in Android from Google).

Unlike Bill Gates, Linus is not a billionaire, despite Linux running on millions of computers worldwide, but according to research done by Revered by Computer, he is the most famous computer programmer on the planet.

The process of installing Linux became much simpler at the beginning of this century and nowadays everyone can easily install it without any extra computer knowledge as you are going to find out soon. Most Linux distributions nowadays come in Live CD format so you can run it straight from a cd without installing it, without making any changes to your system. This is another thing that neither Windows nor Mac offer.

Linux is also the most popular operating system on Supercomputers. As of 2011, more than 90% of the supercomputers run Linux.

2 Preparations before installing Linux

In most cases when you purchase a new computer, it has Microsoft Windows installed (or Mac OS X if it is a Mac). Most major manufacturers provide computers with an operating system installed. Some of them even install one of the Linux distributions on their machines, but it's still quite rare (or at least in Europe). So in this chapter we'll go through preparing your computer for Linux installation.

If you are like most users, you have a computer that runs Windows or Mac OS already. Now you have two choices:

- you can install Linux on the entire disk and remove your existing operating system

- you can install Linux along the other operating system and have both running

If you decide to install Linux along the other operating system, you will be able to log into them one at a time. If you decide to log into Linux and you are inside Windows, you will need to restart your machine (which shouldn't take long). That's what most people do, they want to keep their other operating system either just in case or maybe because they run some proprietary software on this operating system.

If you run other operation system currently on your computer (I will assume Windows), you will need to create a partition for Linux. One partition for Windows and one for Linux. A partition is just a portion of a disk a bit like a slice on a cake. Before you start installing any operating system, make sure you are prepared. Kubuntu runs on a variety of hardware, but it is worth to check how it is going to run on your computer. That's why I am thrilled to let you know that you can check Linux out before you install it! You just simply run it from a cd. As simple as that! And if everything is working and you are happy with what you see, you can start installation! We'll get to that in just a few moments.

Back to partitioning, you will need to create a partition for Linux. If you currently run Windows 7 it's really easy. So what we are going to create here is a configuration often called a "dual-boot". When you start your computer you will be able to choose which operating system you want to run. So let's get to work!

Creating a partition for Linux on Windows

I'm only going to show you how to create a new partition on Windows 7. For any other operating system, do a bit of search online and you'll find how to do it. It's really easy.

1 First you need to shrink the partition from the free space to create new unallocated space on the disk to use it to create a new partition. You will use Disk Management for that.

2 Go to Start menu > Control Panel.

3 In the Control Panel click on view drop-down menu and set it to Large Icons (on the right hand side), then choose Administrative Tools and Computer Management.

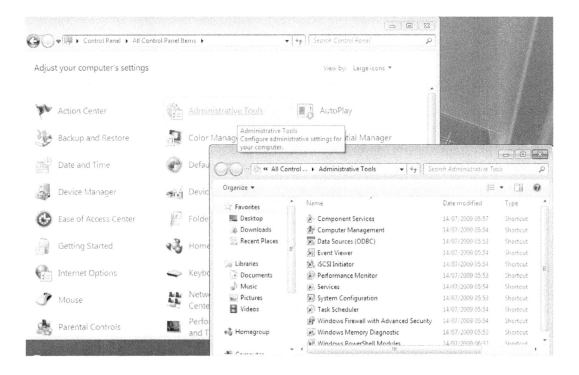

The screenshot on this page above shows you the Administrative Tools in Windows 7.

4 In the Computer Management dialogue box click on Disk Management under Storage.

5 In the centre right click on the empty unallocated space and choose New Simple Volume.

6 New Simple Volume Wizard will open to guide you through the steps.

7 In the Specify Volume Size step you'll need to specify how much space you want to use for the unallocated partition. Just think how much space you want to leave for existing Windows installation and assign the rest to Linux or you may want to divide your hard drive in half.

(NOTE: Windows will display the maximum disk space you can assign to the new partition).

8 In the next step assign an available letter to the partition and finally type the Volume Label name that you want to use (I called mine Linux) and then Finish!

9 The new partition will now be created to you can close the Computer Management window to exit.

Now that you have created a new partition for Linux, you're ready to go! You're going to reboot your computer and install it now.

3 Linux Installation using Kubuntu 11.04

During the installation process Kubuntu will install a loader called GRUB on your hard drive so that you could choose which operation system you want to start when starting the computer (if you have one operating system installed already and you want to keep it). But first, you're going to start your computer from a CD.

Most computers can be started from a CD. You could do it by setting your BIOS to boot from CD, but most computers will give you a quick access to Boot Menu as the computer starts (you will usually see the computer manufacturer's logo when you start the computer and there should be a keyboard shortcut on the screen, i.e. on Dell laptops it's in the corner of the screen and it's the F12 keyboard shortcut to access Boot Menu).

The screenshot on the next page show the example on my laptop:

Once you access the Boot Menu, select the CD/DVD and with the disc inside your drive press OK on your keyboard.

Now, when your computer starts from a CD, you should see a new screen with a few options as shown on the screenshot on the next page:

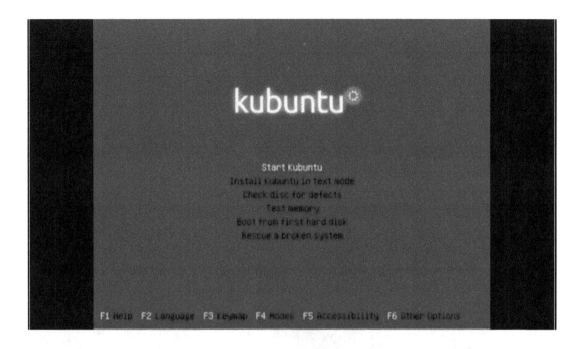

Here are some of the options as shown on the screenshot:

- **Start Kubuntu** – this option allows you to start Kubuntu from the disc without making any changes to your operating system (one of the amazing features of Linux that cannot be found on other operating systems, you start it from the disc, see if you like it and then decide whether you want to install it, pretty impressive).

- **Install Kubuntu in text mode** – this mode allows you to install Kubuntu and perform certain specialist installations.

- **Check disc for defects** – you can check the disk for any problems/defects before you start installing Linux. If it detects any errors on the disc, you may want to decide to download the fresh Linux installation from the vendors website.

- Test Memory – you can run a check on the memory to see if any RAM memory chip is faulty so you could replace it.

- Boot from first hard disk – you can use this option if you left the CD in the drive unintentionally and you want to just start your currently installed operating system.

The option you're going to use here is to start Linux (the first option), so just select this option and press Enter on your keyboard.

Linux will now start by loading all the components from the CD into your computer's memory (RAM) and in just a moment you will be presented with the KDE desktop environment.

You can now decide whether you want to try it first or install it as shown on the screenshot below:

If you are testing Linux first, remember that Linux loads from the disk into your computer's memory so performance won't be the same as if you had Linux already installed. It is designed to just give you a taste of what Linux is like and so that you could test your hardware, check if all your hardware works (this is something people who never used Linux are afraid of). If something doesn't work (it may happen), don't panic and maybe do some research online to see how to fix it. Someone may have had the same issue before and they may have fixed it.

NOTE: If you are having issues with anything, one of the great places to go is the Ubuntu Forums (if you are going to use Ubuntu or Kubuntu).

You can find it at: *http://ubuntuforums.org*. You will find me on Ubuntu Forums quite often as well, so if you come say Hello. You'll find me as *marer13*.

Once you've decided to start installing Linux, click on Install Kubuntu to start the process.

After a few seconds you will be prompted to select the language (you can choose among many different languages, even including Welsh! ;-)).

If you then click Forward, you'll be prompted to check a few things before you start installation process:

- You will need at least 7.5GB of available space

- You should be plugged in to a power source

- You should be connected to the Internet (with a cable, your wireless won't work yet)

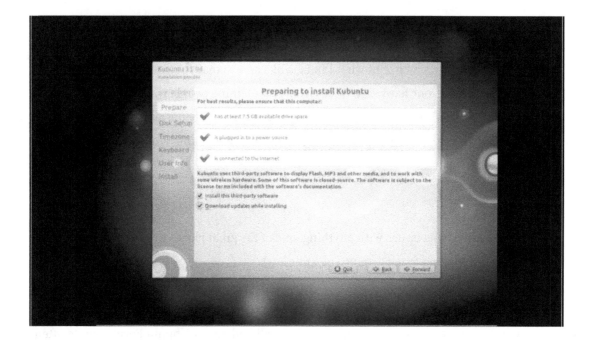

If these conditions are met, you will see green ticks next to them. Near the bottom of the screen there are a few more interesting options:

- *Install third-party software*

- *Download updates while installing*

Both options sound like a good idea. Third-party software might be proprietary software like Adobe Flash Player or sound/video codecs.

You can click Forward to move to the next screen.

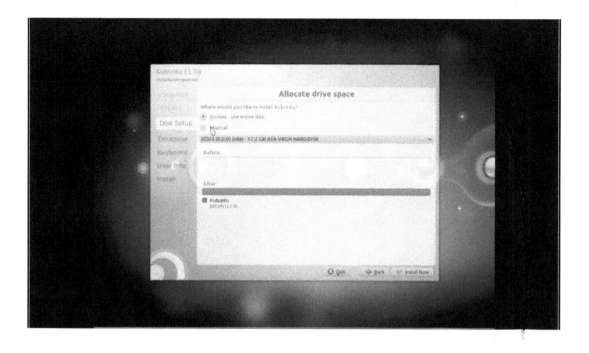

Now the next step is the Disk Setup. In this step you need to allocate disk space to Linux. Leaving it as Guided is usually a good idea (and it is the easiest option, best option if you don't have any Linux experience). If you have Windows or Mac installed on the same machine, Guided will select the empty partition for Linux, so you just leave it as Guided and click Install Now.

When you click Install Now, Linux will start installing (you are going to see a progress bar on the top of the window). At the same time you are going to see another screen in just a few seconds.

This will be the Timezone screen, where you can choose your Timezone, where you live:

Select your location and press Forward again to go to the next screen – Keyboard (Linux will keep on installing as you go through these screens).

As you choose your location, Linux will automatically set your keyboard to match your location, i.e. I've selected United Kingdom as my location and the keyboard that appeared on the Keyboard screen was set automatically to English (UK).

The next screen is User Info as shown below:

On this screen, you are going to add following information:

Your name – this could be anything you want, I usually type in here *marer13* (that's my nickname I use online, if you ever want to find me anywhere online, whether it's flickr or google+, that's how you find me)

Pick a username – this will be your username, when logging in into your system

Choose password – a password obviously, required to log in since the beginning of Linux (something that was only recently introduced in Windows)

Your computer's name – this name will appear when you use Bluetooth, that's how the devices will recognise it, or when on network, again this could be anything, I usually leave it as Linux suggests

Require my password to log in – if you don't want to log in automatically (the option next to it), you will need to type in your password to access your system.

I recommend checking this box even if you're the only person using the computer. Keep your Linux safe.

Encrypt my home folder – you can encrypt your home folder, so it would be more difficult to get access to it even if someone gets access to your computer. I normally don't use it, so don't use it unless you're very paranoid.

Ok, you're done here, so you can click Forward.

This will bring another screen – Install. Now you don't have to do anything, just watch Linux installing and you can read a bit more about Linux and other Open-source software as shown on the screenshot below:

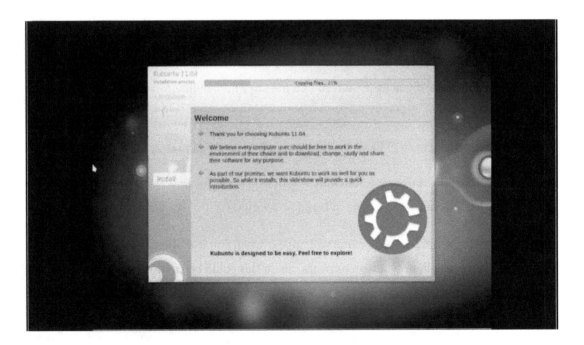

The installation process shouldn't take long. As you can see from my screenshot, it is copying some files already (it reads **Copying files... 21%**).

Once it's done, you'll be presented with a final screen notifying you about the successful installation as shown below:

So, now the final step of installation – Restarting your computer. You've successfully accomplished Linux installation! Well done! You deserve a treat!

Click Restart Now to restart your computer and boot into your brand new Linux.

NOTE: When your computer starts, if you have other operating systems installed on the same computer, you will see a screen with all operating systems listed. Linux will be the first option on the top, so you can press Enter, or if you do nothing, Linux will load automatically after 5 seconds.

In just a moment you will see the login screen (if you checked Require my password to log in), so type in your user name and a password and in just a few second you will see how KDE loads your desktop:

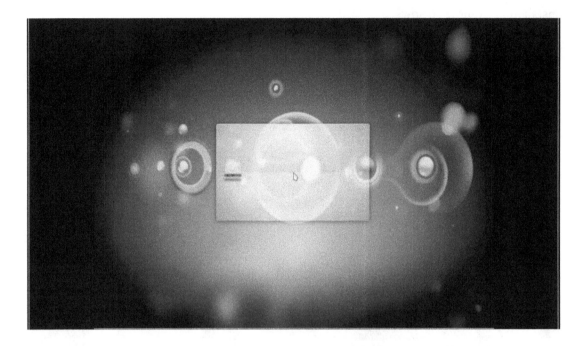

Your desktop (in this case KDE) loads all the required components.

This should only take a few seconds and in just a moment you will be presented with your brand new Linux desktop as shown on the next page!

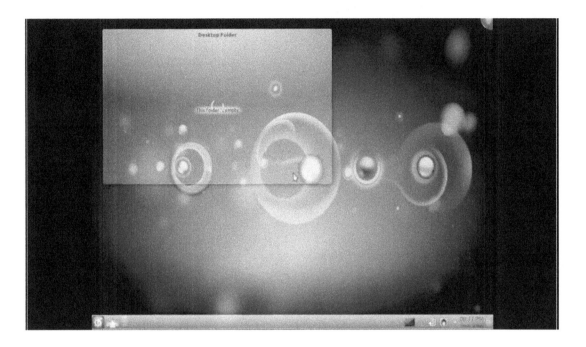

Welcome to your Linux desktop! You made it!

Now, you're ready to move to the next chapter and start exploring your Linux desktop.

4 Exploring your Linux desktop

Now that you have installed Linux successfully it is time for some post-installation configuration and getting acquainted with Linux desktop environment. If you are moving to Linux from Windows or Mac OS, one of the challenges for many users is to find comparable software on Linux, so I'm going to give you Linux equivalents to Windows applications in a chapter near the end of the book.

Linux taskbar and Start menu

Looking at your new desktop environment, notice the familiar taskbar with the start menu at the bottom of the screen.

In this chapter you're going to customise your new operating system. In this chapter you're going to get quickly up to speed with Linux so that by the end of the chapter you'll feel comfortable enough.

A few words about the taskbar, or "panel" as it's often called in KDE "slang". It appears across the bottom of your screen by default and it can easily be repositioned. I will show you how to move it to the top and then install the dock at the bottom of the screen as I always do.

The start button in the taskbar appears in the left corner of the taskbar (like on Windows) and it has a KDE logo:

Next to the Start button there is a:

- *Quick Launch section* and

- *Virtual Desktops* (by default two, I changed it to four).

To customise the taskbar, right-click on it and choose **Panel Options > Panel Settings**.

Now, if you want to move the taskbar to the top of the screen as I did, click on Screen Edge, hold the mouse button down and drag it to the top of the screen. Then release the mouse button and Voila! Done! Your taskbar should now appear on the top of the screen.

To access more options to customise the taskbar, click on More Settings button on the right side of the panel (if you don't see the More Settings button right-click on the taskbar again and choose Panel Options > Panel Settings). Once you click on More Settings you'll see this window:

In here you can decide whether you want to keep the taskbar visible all the time (I do) or whether you want to set it to Auto-hide. All options here are self-explanatory. When done, just click anywhere on the desktop to close it.

To access applications, just click on the Start button and then Applications:

As you can see from the screenshot, applications on Linux are grouped into categories.

This means that if you are looking for a web browser like Firefox, look under Internet as shown on the screenshot on this page below:

Now, let's move on to talking about the Virtual Desktops in Linux, one of my (many) favourite features in Linux.

Virtual Desktops

This is one of the great features in Linux, and one of my favourites, that is not found in Windows. It is the ability to run multiple "virtual" desktops to separate work.
Let me give you an example :

on desktop 1 you run your email client,

on desktop 2 a web browser, and

on desktop 3 you edit images or videos.

By default when you install Kubuntu you get two virtual desktops represented by two buttons next to the Start button. To add more virtual desktops, right-click on one of the virtual desktops and choose Add Virtual Desktop as shown below:

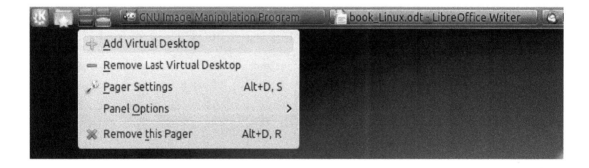

If you do it twice, you'll have four desktop as I have here. The active desktop is highlighted (on my screen it's desktop 4). Clicking on the desktop icon will slide to another desktop.

By default, there is no transition between the desktops, you just see the content on another desktop. Let me show you how to activate the cube animation, very cool effect!

Right-click on one of the desktops and choose Pager Settings. This will open the Pager Settings dialogue box as shown below:

Click on the Virtual Desktops category on the left to see the options as displayed on the screenshot on the next page:

In here you can decide on how many virtual desktops you want to have (another way of adding new virtual desktops) and you can give them names if you want.

Switch to **Switching** tab on the top to change how to move between the virtual desktops:

Change Animation to Desktop Cube Animation. Don't press OK yet. I'll show you the keyboard shortcuts you can use to move between the virtual desktops.

In the bottom part of the dialogue box there is a section for **Shortcuts**.

Under **Action** find **Desktop Switching > Switch to Desktop 1** etc.

Notice the keyboard shortcuts. From now on, you can enjoy using the keyboard shortcuts! Now press OK and try it out! Have fun, it really is fun!

NOTE: (people are usually impressed when I show them this feature and they wish they could do it in Windows).

Desktop Background

In this section you're going to get acquainted with your desktop background. You're not going believe it how easy it is to customise your desktop background.

Just right-click anywhere on your desktop and choose **Desktop Settings** (I told you it's easy...).

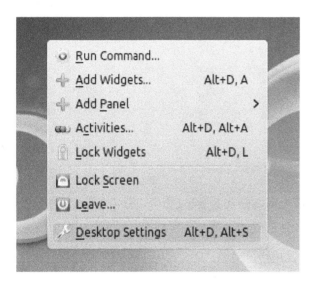

In the dialogue box that opens, click **Open** and navigate to the file that you want to use, it can be a JPEG, PNG, SVG, BMP.

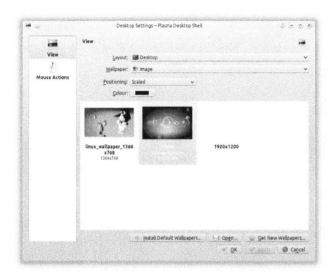

Then click OK (or Apply to preview the change first) and that's it!

You have successfully changed your desktop background. Congratulations!

Screen Resolution

When you start Linux, it automatically detects the best resolution for your screen. However, sometimes you may want to change your screen resolution, maybe lower it a bit, so you may want to know how to do it. That's what this part of this chapter is about.

To change the screen resolution you need to access the Display Settings.

Go to the **Start** button and choose: **Applications > System > Screen Resize & Rotate (KrandRTray)**.

In just a few seconds you should see the monitor icon on the taskbar:

Click on it and it will open **Display Settings** dialogue box like the one shown below:

In **Display Settings** dialogue box you can set the resolution of your screen as well as a refresh rate.

NOTE: If you connect your computer to an external monitor or projector, the Display Settings dialogue box will appear automatically so you could set the options for both displays.

That's what the sections below are for:

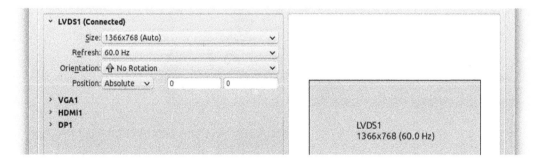

Change your Screen Saver and Power Options

NOTE: Power Options for laptops

Now that you've set your screen resolution, it is time to change the screensaver and set the Power Options.

To change your Screen Saver, you'll need to access the System Settings:
Start > Applications > System > System Settings.

In the System Settings dialogue box click on **Display and Monitor** under **Hardware**:

In the Display and Monitor dialogue box there are three categories on the left hand side, one of them is **Screen Saver**.

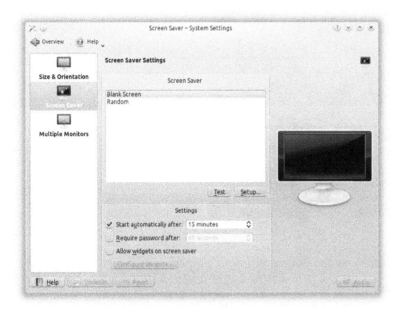

Choose the Screen Saver you want to use and decide when you want it to start next by setting an option next to **Start Automatically after:**. Click **Apply** and close the dialogue box.

Now the **Power Settings**, where you will be able to decide when you want Linux to go into **Powersave Mode** etc.

Click on the battery icon in the taskbar and you'll see the dialogue box as shown below:

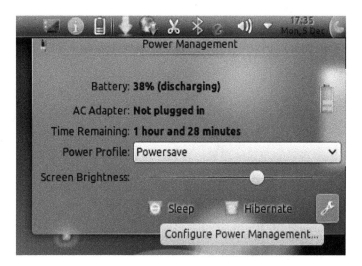

In the bottom right corner you'll see the Configure Power Management icon (it looks like a wrench - shown on the screenshot above).

Click on it to open the **Power Management** dialogue box:

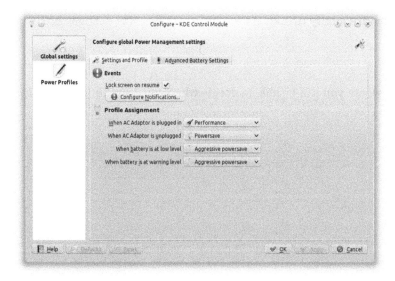

In the **Settings and Profile** tab set the options to the same options as on the screenshot above (you can change them later on).

Basically, what you want to do here is:

- use the maximum power from your computer when it runs from the mains

   (**Performance – When AC Adaptor is plugged in**), and

- save the battery life when it runs on battery so that you can run it longer

   (**Powersave – When AC Adaptor is unplugged**).

When the battery reaches low level and When battery is at warning level, you'll use **Aggresive powersave** to use the laptop on battery for as long as you can.

Go to the **Advanced Battery Settings** tab:

In here you can set when you want the battery to start using **Aggresive Powersave Mode** (when the battery is at low and warning level (if you set the low level to launch Powersave mode not Aggresive Powersave mode in the Settings and Profile tab, these two: Battery is at low level and Battery is at warning level will make a difference).

When done, just click OK to save and exit.

Update your software

One of the first things you should do upon successfully installing your new operating system is to install any new updates. They usually bring some security updates and bug fixes. If there are new updates, the update manager should appear in your taskbar. If it doesn't you can access it from the menu. Let me show you how.

Go to the **Start** menu, then:

Applications > System > Software Management (KPackageKit):

In just a few seconds **KpackageKit** application will open and you will see three categories on the left:

Get and Remove Software,

Software Updates, and

Settings.

Let's start with the Settings category.

Click on Settings and you'll see the following dialogue box:

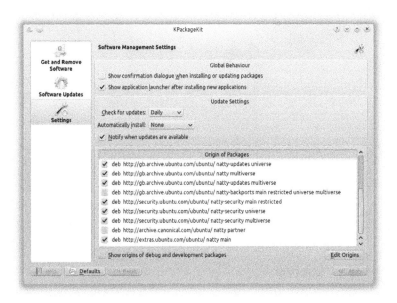

That's where you can check and add the origins of the packages (whether you want to get updates only from Ubuntu-approved sources or from any other sources). The important thing here right now is the option **Notify when updates are available**. Make sure it's checked (it should be by default). You can also decide how often you want to check for updates (I left it as daily) and whether you want to install updates automatically.

Now let's move on to the Software Updates category:

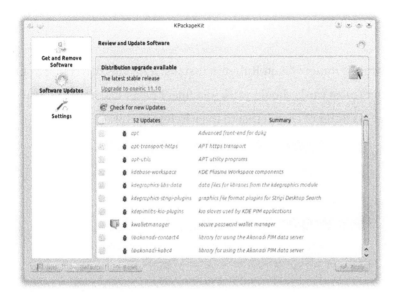

Software Updates category is the section within the KpackageKit, where you can find all available updates to your software.

If you want to install any of the updates, just click in the box next to it and then click Apply. You will be prompted for your password before you install anything, so remember about your password.

Get your wireless connection

It is time to connect to the wireless router. When Kubuntu installs, it installs drivers for your wireless card in your computer (most cards should work just fine, I never had any troubles with wireless). So now it's just a matter of connecting to the wireless router.

In your taskbar find the wireless connection icon and click on it.

Click the **Show More...** button to see all wireless networks in your area:

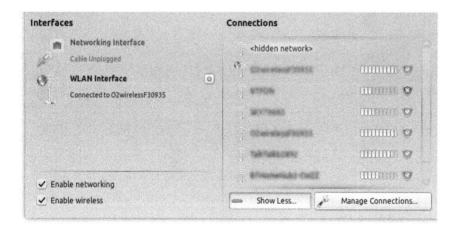

When you find your network, click on its name to connect to it. **Add Network Connection** dialogue box will appear and you'll need to type the password. Also, if it's a network you use a lot (like your home or work network), check **Connect Automatically**. Next time you're in range, Linux will connect to your network automatically.

When done just press OK.

NOTE: If you're having any troubles connecting to the router wirelessly, contact your internet provider for help connecting(they should have provided you with the router).

5 Get up to speed with Linux

Get started with a Web Browser - Firefox

Everyone is connected to the internet nowadays and the web browser is one of the most often used applications. There are many web browsers out there and one of the most popular ones is Mozilla Firefox. Firefox is also installed with Kubuntu, so you can start using it straight away.

Firefox is a great alternative to Internet Explorer for Windows users and since its beginning in 2004 it reached a very big market share (at the moment of writing – Dec 2011 – it is the second most popular web browser with around 42% market share worldwide. One of the many reasons behind the huge popularity of Firefox is a wealth of extensions and plug-ins, as well as many multimedia codecs.

To access Firefox go to **Start menu > Applications > Internet > Firefox**. As you start it for the first time, you'll be prompted to go through the quick start up process and in just a moment you can start enjoy surfing the web.

Here's what Firefox looks like on Linux (very similar to what you may have seen on Windows or Mac OS):

Get started with an Email Client – Thunderbird

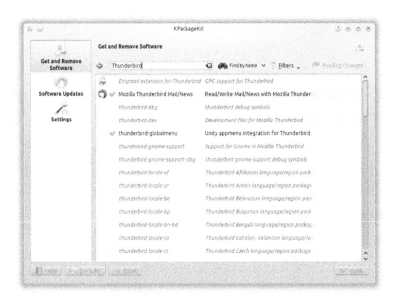

There are a number of email clients out there and you may have used some Windows-based email clients in the past. Some of them are cross-platform so they work on both Windows and Linux (and even Mac OS) and one of them is Mozilla Thunderbird – an email client developed by the same Mozilla Foundation organisation that developed Firefox.

Thunderbird is not installed with Kubuntu by default, so you'll need to install it yourself but it's a very straightforward process.

To install Thunderbird go to **Start > Applications > System > Software Management**. When KPackageKit opens, type **Thunderbird** in the search box at the top and press Enter:

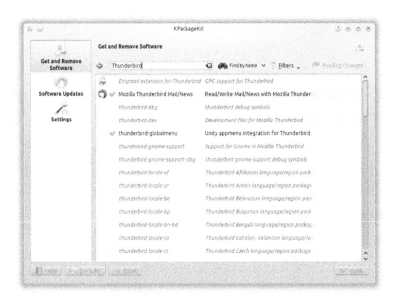

Highlight Thunderbird and click Install next to it on the right hand side.

Next click **Apply** at the bottom of the screen.

To install it, you'll be prompted for your password, so just type it and press Enter on your keyboard.

The installation shouldn't take long (it depends on your internet connection as the packages are going to be downloaded and then installed) and you will see a dialogue box from which you can launch Thunderbird.

You can close KpackageKit.

Once you have Thunderbird installed, launch it. When Thunderbird launches, you will be able to set up your email.

You should see the following dialogue box:

NOTE: At any time you can invoke this dialogue box by clicking on **Create New Account** in the main window in Thunderbird or alternatively choose **File > New > Mail Account...** as shown on the screenshots on the next page:

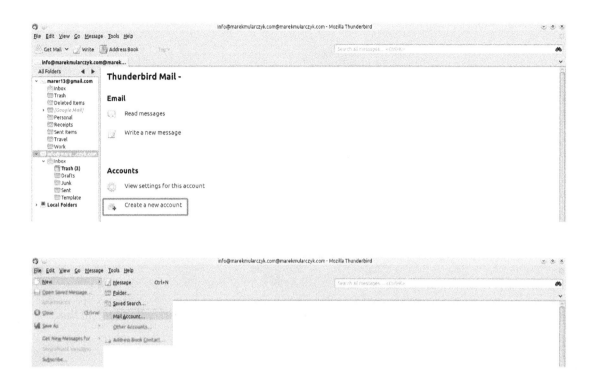

Next, just follow the instructions. If you have an email account with a well known provider like Google, setting up your email account is quick and easy, Thunderbird will do all the work required to set it up for you. If you use a less known email provider, check with them, they may provide you with a script to quickly set up your email with Thunderbird.

Here's how it works with Gmail:

When you type your Gmail email address and your password, Thunderbird will fill all the details for you as shown on the screenshot above.

NOTE: If you want to keep your emails on your server so you could access them at any time from any computer, set your incoming server to **IMAP** (as shown on the screenshot above). If you set the incoming server to POP, Thunderbird will download all your emails and you won't be able to read them on another computer (at work or in internet cafe).

I personally use IMAP as I access my email on my mobile phone, laptop, or sometimes internet cafe.

Here's a screenshot showing how I can quickly set up Thunderbird with my email provider from within the control panel:

Email Account ⇩	Catch-all	Forward	Anti-Spam	Auto-Config	Auto-responder	Password
info@marekmularczyk.com		♀ ⊞				
info@saitraining.co.uk		♀ ⊞				
test@marekmularczyk.com		♀ ⊞				

Automatically apply your mailbox settings to a Mozilla Thunderbird e-mail client.

Once you're done setting up your email, you will see it in the left pane as shown below:

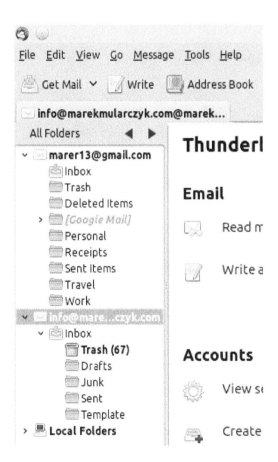

You can set up multiple emails with Thunderbird as shown here I have two emails set up in Thunderbird.

To get emails, click **Get Mail** button in the top left corner of Thunderbird interface:

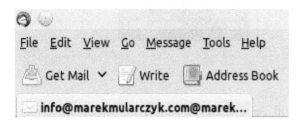

NOTE: Thunderbird automatically checks for new emails when you open it.

Install a Printer

Every computer user has different needs when it comes to using a computer. However, more often than not you are going to want to print something, so you will need to install a printer. Installing a printer on Linux may be a different experience from other operating systems.

Let me tell you this first: installing a printer may be a straightforward process, in many cases you won't even need to install any drivers (unlike on other operating systems). However, some printers are not that easily supported. Support for printers on Linux varies and it is not a Linux fault, it's just that printers' manufacturers do not create drivers for Linux, they usually only support Windows and Mac.

So, if you know you are going to use Linux most of the time and you are buying a new printer, do some research online and see which ones work best.

NOTE: From my own experience with the printers I have used in the past, HP and Samsung worked great for me. On the other hand, from what I have heard, Lexmark printers have really bad reputation when it comes to installing them on Linux.

Here's a great website that may help. You can check here if your printer will work on Linux:

OpenPrinting.org – Printer database.

Here's how you install a printer on Linux:

1 Turn the printer on and connect it to the computer.

2 Open System Settings: **Start menu** > **Applications** > **Settings** > **System Settings**

3 In the System Settings dialogue box click on **Printer Configuration** under **Hardware**.

4 This will open Printer Configuration dialogue box, on the left click on **New Printer**.

5 On the right click on **New Printer** button:

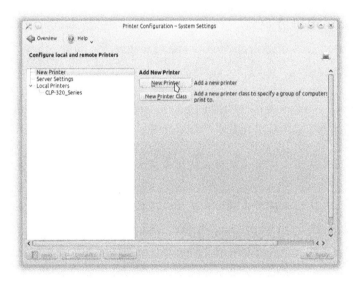

Because you have connected the printer to your computer, Linux will now try to detect it and point you to the right device driver.

Here's what came up when I connected my Samsung CLP-325W laser printer to my laptop:

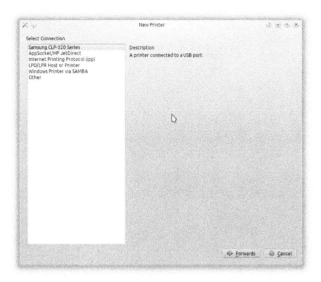

6 If the connection is detected properly, just click **Forwards** and in the next screen choose the brand of the printer:

7 Click Forwards and on the next screen choose the model (if your model doesn't appear, choose a similar model from the same line, i.e. I here chose CLP-315 instead of CLP-325):

8 Click **Forwards** and give your printer a name that will appear in the Print dialogue box and a description if you want. When done, click OK.

You're done! Congratulations! You can now close the Printer Configuration dialogue box and start printing.

From now on, when you choose to print something, the printer will appear in the drop-down menu in the Print dialogue box.

Call over Internet with Ekiga

Ekiga is an Internet videoconferencing application that you can use to call using the Internet connection. It provides voice and picture transmission so you can chat to your friends using a webcam or you can call phone numbers (landline and mobile).

To install Ekiga, go to **Start > Applications > System > Software Management**. When KPackageKit opens, type **Ekiga** in the search box at the top and install it following the same step as in the previous chapters.

Once Ekiga is installed, you will find it under:

Start > Applications > Internet > IP Telephony, VoIP and Video Conferencing:

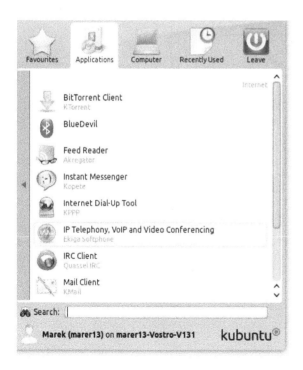

When you start it for the first time, the configuration wizard will launch to guide you through the setup. Just follow the steps and start using Ekiga in a matter of minutes!

If you want to use Ekiga to make phone calls over the internet (I use it to call family), here's what to do:

1 Register with one of the VoIP providers

2 Start Ekiga and go to **Edit > Accounts**.

3 Click **Accounts > Add a SIP Account**.

4 Fill all the fields in the dialogue box (settings will depend on your provider, contact them if needed) and click **OK**.

5 When done, you can start making phone calls, to many landlines for free. Just type the number and click on the green icon:

Get to know the File Manager

Dolphin is the default File Manager in Kubuntu. It is the default File Manager in most KDE distributions.

Dolphin offers a lot of functionality and it's fast and lightweight at the same time. Here's what it looks like:

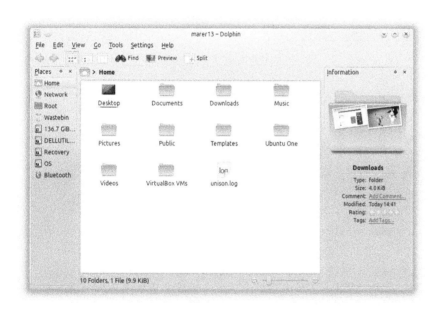

Let's have a look at the interface (on the next page):

on the left – shortcuts to places like Home and any USB devices connected to the computer. You can drag and drop files into this part of the File Manager

on the top – back and forward buttons, view modes, Find, Preview and Split

in the centre – main workspace, where all folders and files appear

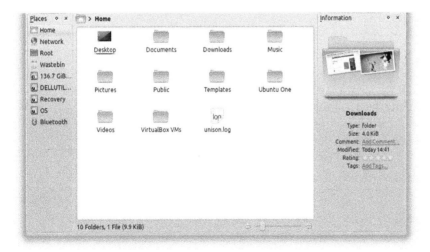

NOTE: Single click opens folders and files (not double-click like in Windows), if you want to highlight a folder or file, hold down Ctrl key and click.

Home Directory

If you haven't used Linux before, Home directory will be something new to you.

Home directory is used to store personal data. Every user in Linux has its own Home directory and this is where you store your documents, music, images, videos etc. It's like My Documents directory in Windows.

Create a New Folder

Now, let me show you how to create a new folder. Click on Documents folder to open it as shown below:

When the Documents folder opens, choose **File > Create New > Folder...**

When New Folder dialogue box opens, give your new folder a name and press OK:

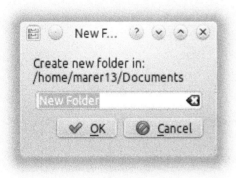

Alternatively to create a new folder you can right-click in the empty space inside the folder and choose **Create New > Folder...**

Now, you're going to connect a USB memory and copy some files.

Copying Files and using USB memory

You're going to start by connecting (mounting) a USB memory to your computer.

1 Plug it in and in just a moment you'll see it appear in the taskbar in the drop-down menu like that:

2 Click on the name of the USB device to see available options:

3 Click **Open with File Manager** and the File Manager will open displaying the content of your USB device:

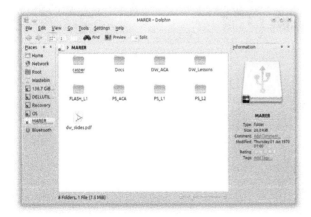

4 If you missed the drop-down menu (it only appears for a few seconds), click on the USB icon in the taskbar to get access to your USB device:

NOTE: Notice a very interesting feature in Linux – when you roll over the name of your USB device you're going to see how much space you have left on it! Very cool!:

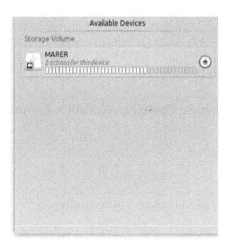

5 In the File Manager that opens select the file (or files) you want to copy by holding down **Ctrl** key and clicking on them.

6 Then release the Ctrl key and right-click on one of the files highlighted and choose **Copy**:

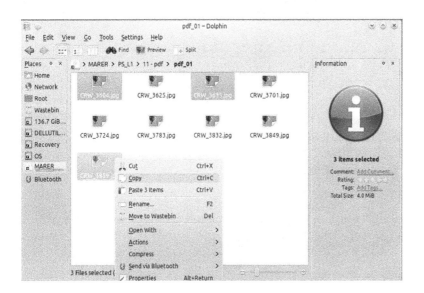

7 In the shortcuts to places on the left click on **Home** and **Documents**.

8 When the **Documents folder** opens, right-click and choose **Paste** (or use **Edit > Paste**) to paste the files.

If you're not going to use the USB drive any more, you will need to eject it (you could just remove it manually from the USB port, but to make sure you don't loose any data on it, it's a good practise to unmount it in Linux).

9 Click on the USB icon in the taskbar, roll your cursor over the your device's icon and click on Eject icon on the right:

Alternatively you can also right-click on the USB device icon in the File Manager and choose **Safely Remove...**:

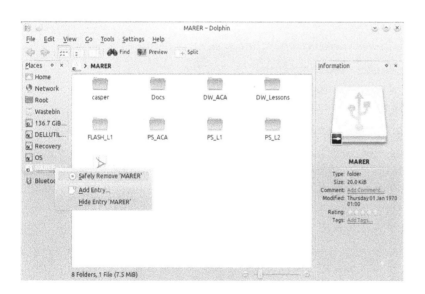

Linux Directories Guide

If you are a new user that moved to Linux from Windows, you need to be aware of some differences between the operating systems.

Here are some things to have in mind:

- Linux is a case-sensitive operating system, Windows is not, i.e. Linux will treat "image.txt" and "IMAGE.txt" as two seperate files

- Linux doesn't use letters for drives like Windows, i.e. on Windows the primary hard drive is C:, CD/DVD drive is D: or E: etc

- Linux was created as a multi-user network operating system, unlike Windows which evolved from DOS as a single-user operating system for home users

- Linux users cannot change system settings, only a super user (root) can, you'll be prompted for a password to change system settings. Windows users can easily change system settings without any passwords.

- Linux uses a different file system from Windows: Linux – ext3, Windows – FAT32 or NTFS.

NOTE: The differences in file systems do not mean that you cannot copy the files between Windows and Linux (using a USB memory as an example). Linux understands FAT32 and NTFS formatted USB devices.

Lack of drive letters in Linux (and Mac OS) is one of the big differences between Windows and Linux/Mac OS. There is a hierarchy in Linux – a tree directory – beginning with the root directory indicated by a slash (/).

Here's the directory tree in the File Manager:

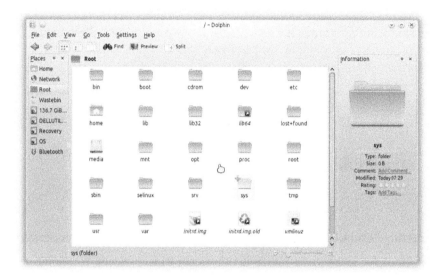

And here's a quick overview of the directories:

bin - this directory contains executable programs. It contains the important programs that the system needs to operate

boot - this is the directory that contains the heart of the Linux operating system – the Linux kernel. Linux kernel is typically called 'vmlinuz'.

etc - this directory contains system configuration files, i.e. user passwords, screen resolution settings, etc

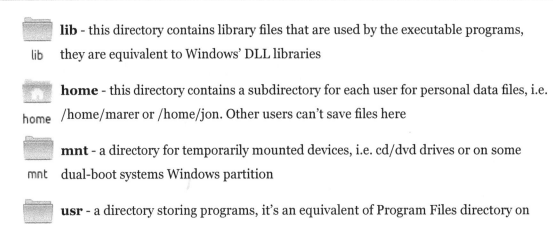

lib - this directory contains library files that are used by the executable programs, they are equivalent to Windows' DLL libraries

home - this directory contains a subdirectory for each user for personal data files, i.e. /home/marer or /home/jon. Other users can't save files here

mnt - a directory for temporarily mounted devices, i.e. cd/dvd drives or on some dual-boot systems Windows partition

usr - a directory storing programs, it's an equivalent of Program Files directory on Windows

Compress and Extract Files

Compressing and extracting files in Linux is very easy. And the good news is that compressing files has been a part of Linux for many years unlike in other operating systems. You don't need to install any software to start compressing files or folders!

There are three main compressing formats:

zip, *rar*, and *tar*.

Tar is a very popular in Linux, it is often used for transferring files.

Compressing files/folders is really easy.

1 Select a file or folder that you want to compress and right-click on it.

2 In the drop-down menu that appears choose **Compress** > and choose one of the formats. That's it! Have a look at the screenshot below:

In just a moment you're going to have a new compressed file as shown on the screenshot below:

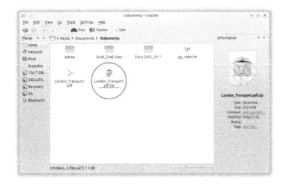

The original Pdf file is 260kB and the compressed version is 215kB. Of course you can compress entire folders, i.e. an entire folder with images so that you could easily email them etc. Sometimes we compress files not just to get them to be smaller (in terms of file size), but for example so that they're easier to email (it is easier to email one file instead of ten or twenty).

To uncompress a file or folder, you can right-click on it and choose **Extract Archive To...** or **Extract Archive Here**:

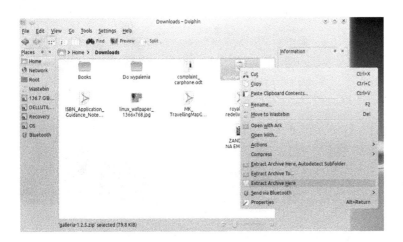

If you want to see the contents of the archive before you extract it or maybe you want to extract just one of the files in the archive, just click on it and the archive will open in Ark as shown on the next page:

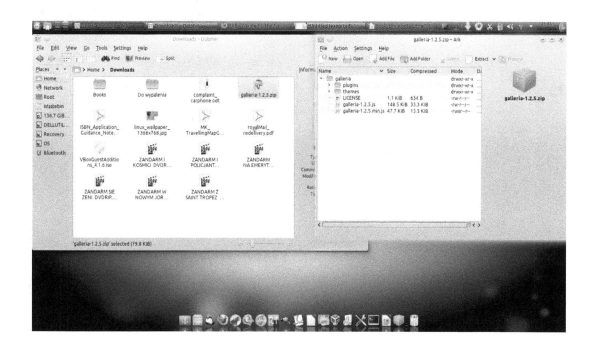

6 Get productive with Linux

A dock with Docky

Installation

Docky is a great dock application for Linux. It is widely known as the most user friendly dock application available in Linux. It gives you quick access to the most often used applications installed on your computer. Here's what it looks like on the desktop:

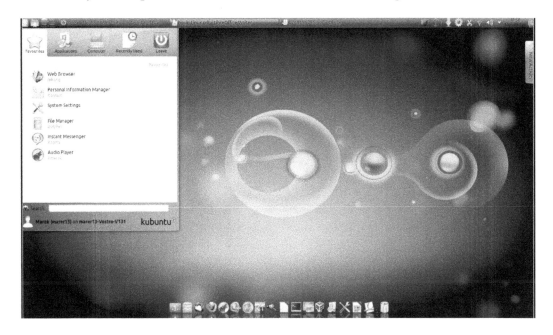

And here's what it looks like in a close-up:

It is very simple and easy to use as well as lightweight.

First you need to install it, so go to the **KpackageKit** and type **Docky** in the search box. Accept it, install it and start using it in a matter of minutes. Once it's installed, launch it and it should appear on the bottom of your screen.

Customise the dock

To customise Docky, click on the Docky icon on the left edge of the dock:

This will open the Docky Settings dialogue box:

In here you can customise the dock. Start with choosing the theme you'd like for your dock. Here are a few examples of themes:

Classic:

Air:

HUD:

Transparent:

Choose the theme from the drop-down menu (choose the one that suits you).

Next, you've got the Dock Configuration section within the same dialogue box.

That's where you can configure hiding behaviour, i.e. you can set dock to hide automatically and reappear when the cursor moves close to the edge.

Here's the drop-down menu:

And here's what the options do:

None – the dock will always be visible

Autohide – the dock will always hide unless you move your cursor over the area where the dock resides (bottom of the screen)

Intellihide - will hide the dock when an application is opened and the dock is obstructing the application. When an application is closed or resized the dock will reappear.

Window Dodge – the dock will hide if it obstructs any window

I like Intellihide and that's the setting I use. If you want the dock to appear all the time, set Hiding to None.

In the next section below the Hiding drop-down menu, you can set the zoom (how big do you want the icons to become when you place your cursor over them) and you may want to check 3D Background (very nice feature, it looks very impressive).

When done, click **Close**.

Add an application to the dock

Here's how you can add an application to the dock.

With the dock running, go to the **Start** menu and find an application you want to add.

Once you find it, click on it and holding the mouse button down drag it onto the dock.

As you move the cursor over the dock, the icons on the dock will move to make place for the new icon and the plus sign (+) will appear next to your cursor (screenshot below, the plus sign appears on the edge of the screen):

When happy with the position of the icon, release the mouse button to place it in the dock:

Remove the application icon from the dock

To remove the application icon from the dock just drag it from the dock and drop it anywhere on the desktop. The icon will disappear.

Add a Docklet to the dock (Weather forecast)

1 Start by clicking on the Docky icon on the left edge of the dock:

2 When the **Docky Settings** dialogue box opens, click on **Docklets** tab:

3 Scroll down the list of docklets until you find the Weather docklet:

4 Click the Plus sign (+) to add it to the dock.

5 Click **Close**.

The Weather docklet icon now appears on the right side of the dock.

6 Now, you're going to customise it. Right-click on the icon and choose **Settings**.

7 In the **Weather Configuration** dialogue box, type the name of your town and click Search on the right. When your town appears below, click on it to select it.

8 If you want to use metric units for temperature (Celsius instead of Fahrenheit) check **Use Metric Units** at the bottom of the dialogue box. You can also choose how often you want to update the weather information (I'm fine with the default – 30 minutes) - see the screenshot on the next page:

9 When done, click **Close**.

Look into the dock, you should now see the weather docklet sitting nicely and displaying the temperature for today as shown below:

Move your cursor over the icon to see the description:

Right-click on the icon to see the quick weather forecast for the next three days:

Now, to find the detailed weather forecast, click on the **Weather docklet**.

The dock will be replaced with a detailed weather forecast for the next three days:

Now you can see the temperatures (minimum and maximum) and whether it's going to be sunny or it's going to rain.

On the far right, you will see an arrow icon. Click on it to see more options:

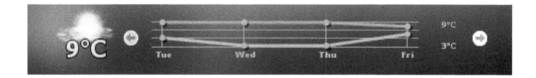

Now, you can see how the temperature is going to change in the next three days (minimum in blue and maximum in red).

Click on the arrow on the far right to get to the next screen:

Now, you can see the detailed information for today:

- from left: temperature, humidity, wind speed and direction, sunrise and sunset.

And that's it for the Weather docklet! A lot of useful information.

To hide the detailed weather information and bring the dock back, click away from the dock.

This is just an example of one of the docklets that you can add to your dock. Feel free to explore additional docklets and customise them on your own, as you have already seen , they're easy to customise.

Finally, for more information about Docky, visit their website:

Docky website – *go-docky.com*.

Create a Text file

Before we jump into office suite, we will create a simple text document. Sometimes you won't need to use an office suite to create a text document and quickly save it.

To create a text file in KDE, you are going to use **Kate**.

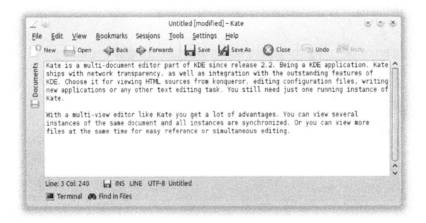

Kate is a document editor part of KDE (Kate stands for KDE Advanced Text Editor) and it ships with Kubuntu (and any other KDE-based Linux distribution).

Start Kate by choosing **Start > Applications > Utilities > Kate**:

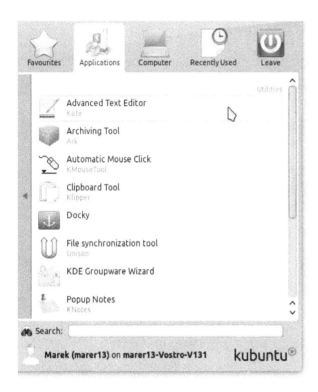

NOTE: If you are having difficulties finding any application, in the Start menu (like the one above) type the name of the application in the Search box near the bottom of the menu and then click on the name of the application that appears at the top.

Back to our text editor, when it opens you can start typing directly (in the same way you would do it in any other text editor).

When done, choose **File > Save As...** :

Give the file a name. Also, choose the location where you want to save the file. Click **Save**:

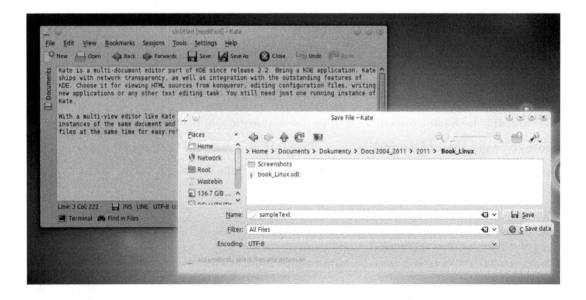

To open the files in Kate use the usual **File > Open**.

File > Open Recent will reveal the names of the files you were recently working on.

Edit menu has the usual **Copy**, **Cut** and **Paste** commands and under **Tools** you will find **Spellcheck**.

Get started with LibreOffice suite

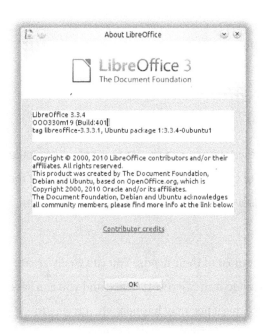

There are many **office suites** out there and many business (as well as personal users) benefited from the development of so many open-source office suites. Many businesses benefit from not having to pay licensing fees for using the office suites when they move away from Microsoft Office and start using **OpenOffice** or **LibreOffice**. Many office suites are available on Linux, we're going to focus on **LibreOffice** as it comes bundled with Kubuntu and many other Linux distributions.

Something I'd like you to understand about **LibreOffice** and **OpenOffice** is that they are not 100% compatible with Microsoft Office and that's because of the proprietary file formats used by Microsoft Office suite. However, **LibreOffice** and **OpenOffice** are highly compatible with Microsoft Office documents and they can easily open **.doc** and **.xls** files as well as save them.

Here are some file formats supported by LibreOffice:

.doc, .docx, .ppt, .pptx, .xls, .xlsx, .rtf,

as well as *Export to PDF and SWF* (Adobe Flash).

You may have been wondering what the term 'office suite' means so let me explain. We talk about an 'office suite' when we deal with a suite of two or more application that are used for creating documents, i.e. text documents, spreadsheets, presentations, databases etc. Some office suites may include an email client as well.

For the majority of users, **LibreOffice** will meet most of their needs. You can easily create documents and spreadsheets in the same way you do it in Microsoft Office and you can save them as .doc and .xls files. The hurdles you may experience may happen when trying to import and/or open files that were created with Microsoft Office (I haven't had any problems so far).

LibreOffice's user interface closely resembles the one of Microsoft Office so you will find switching to LibreOffice very easy. This similarity helps users in switching and they very quickly get used to the new office suite.

Of course, the reason why we're talking about LibreOffice here is not its similarity to Microsoft Office. Benefits of switching to LibreOffice are:

- it's FREE,

- it supports a huge number of file formats, and

- it can export to many different file formats.

LibreOffice consists of many productivity applications used to create documents, spreadsheets, databases, and presentations, and more as shown below:

Here are the components of LibreOffice suite:

LibreOffice Writer – a word processing program used to create and format text documents (equivalent to Microsoft Word).

LibreOffice Calc – a spreadsheet program used to create and format spreadsheets (equivalent to Microsoft Excel).

LibreOffice Impress – a presentation program used to create and customise slideshows (equivalent to Microsoft PowerPoint).

LibreOffice Math – a math formula editor used to write mathematical formulas, includes a number of symbols and math fonts that are not easily included in word processors.

LibreOffice Base – a database program used to create databases (equivalent to Microsoft Access).

Drawing Program
LibreOffice Draw

LibreOffice Draw – a graphics program used to create graphics to be used in the documents created with LibreOffice.

You can access LibreOffice suite by choosing **Start > Applications > Office** as shown below:

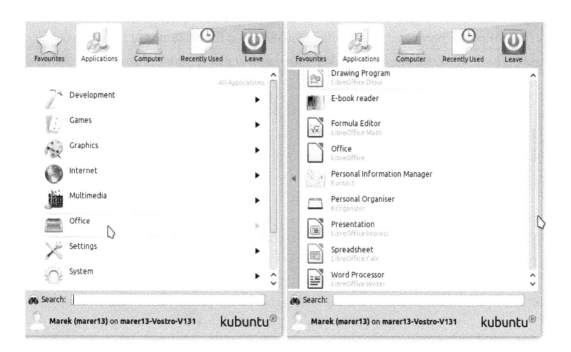

Let me give you **a brief history of LibreOffice**:

LibreOffice has been created by a group called "The Document Foundation" - a group consisting of members of the OpenOffice.org project.

The reason why LibreOffice was formed at the beginning of 2011 was because Oracle Corporation purchased Sun Microsystems (company behind OpenOffice.org) and there were concerns that Oracle would discontinue OpenOffice.org or place restrictions on the development of OpenOffice as an open-source suite as it had done in the past with Sun's OpenSollaris.

In April 2011, Oracle announced terminating the commercial development of OpenOffice.org.

LibreOffice became very popular, since its initial release at the beginning of 2011 it has already been downloaded almost 8 million times (as of end of September 2011).

Create documents in LibreOffice Writer

Start **LibreOffice**: **Start > Applications > Office > Office**, and when LibreOffice launches, click on **Text Document** on the Welcome Screen:

Alternatively, you can choose **File > New > Text Document** from the application menu.

A new blank document opens and you can start adding content.

Once you've typed some text, you can modify it using the Format menu or if you want to change the Font Family or Font Size you can use the drop-down menus at the top of the application frame:

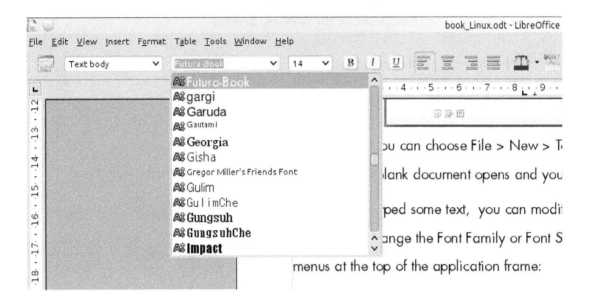

To insert an image into the document, place the cursor where you want the image to appear and choose **Insert > Picture > From File...** as shown on the screenshot on the next page:

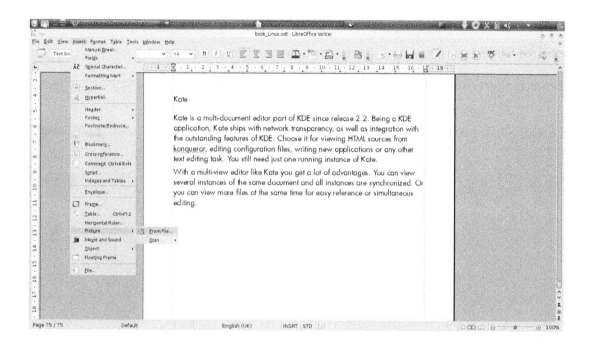

To save your document, choose **File > Save As...** or to save it as a PDF document, choose **File > Export as PDF...**:

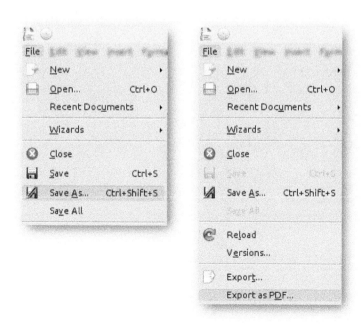

When saving the document, it will by default be saved in the LibreOffice native format with **.odt** file extension.

However, you can save the documents to many file formats as shown on the screenshot here:

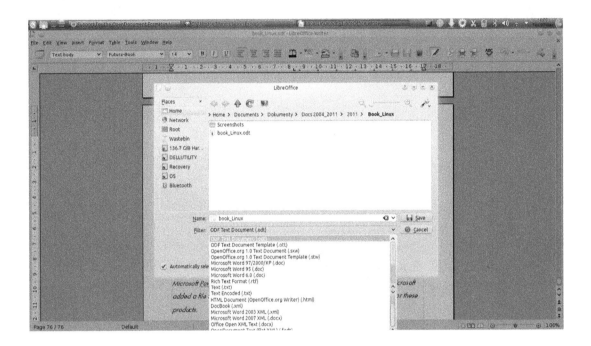

Some of the file formats you can see here are:

- Microsoft Word format - .doc

- Microsoft Word new format - .docx

- Rich Text Format - .rtf

- Text format - .txt

- Microsoft Word XML format - .xml

- and many more

NOTE: Microsoft Office now also supports Open Document Format, so you should be able to open **.odt** or **.ods** files in Microsoft Office – here's what Microsoft says on their website:

Microsoft, as part of its commitment to Interoperability with the European Commission, includes support for ODF 1.1 in Microsoft Excel 2010, Microsoft Word 2010, and Microsoft PowerPoint 2010. With the inclusion of ODF support in Office 2010, Microsoft added a file format selection screen to enable you to select the default file format for these products.

As this is not a book on LibreOffice, this is just an introduction to LibreOffice Writer as an example.

7 Working with graphics

It is very common between Linux users to say that there is a lack of a professional image editor like Photoshop. Adobe Photoshop became an industry standard when it comes to editing graphics. And I can tell you that there is a reason for that. I am not saying that as an Adobe Certified Expert and Instructor in Adobe Photoshop, which I am, but as a user and a photographer. I have used both applications and I can tell you that Photoshop is a real professional graphics editor and I don't think Gimp comes close to what Photoshop can do.

However, some functionality can be achieved with Gimp. If you only open, adjust, save, export images, then you'll be fine with Gimp. Gimp is the most popular free graphics editor on Linux and other platforms, so I'm going to focus on Gimp and show you what it can do.

A few words of introduction. **Gimp – GNU Image Manipulation Program** – is definitely the most popular graphics editor. It also is one of the oldest, if not the oldest. Gimp is not supposed to be a Photoshop imitator, it is different. It's primarily a tool for editing images that will go online or will be printed by a photo lab.

GIMP

Installing GIMP

Gimp may not be installed with Kubuntu, when you install it, so if you can't find it in the **Graphics** applications :

you will need to install it. Just follow the usual steps to install it with a package manager.

Once you have installed Gimp, launch it.

NOTE: If you plan to use it quite a lot, add Gimp launch icon to the dock.

Gimp (like other open-source applications) get updates very often (more often that most proprietary applications), so by the time you're reading this you may be using a newer version of Gimp with some new features.

NOTE: At the time of writing I'm using the unstable version of Gimp - **Gimp 2.7.3**. By the time you read this, the final stable version of Gimp 2.7.3 may be released. If it is not, if you want to use the same version of Gimp, you can download it from Gimp website.

Gimp 2.7.3 is the first version of Gimp working in **Single-Window Mode** (like most graphics editors). What does it mean? Let me show you.

This is the old Gimp mode with floating panels:

And this is the new Gimp **Single-Window Mode**:

You can see that the new **Single-Window Mode** in Gimp gives much clearer interface to work with. All the panels are within the application frame instead of being scattered across the entire desktop.

Single-Window Mode in Gimp is not set by default. To activate it, choose: **Windows > Single-Window Mode**.

Basics of Image editing

To begin with, Gimp looks a bit different from other image editors and some users find it a bit confusing to find which menus do what. That's what I'm going to explain to you here. I will be using the Single-Window Mode as that's what I use on daily basis.

Also, Gimp can open many different file formats, including **JPEG, PNG, GIF**, and **PSD**, and many more.

On the top of the application frame you will find menu as on any other application. Let's start by opening an image. Choose **File > Open** from the menu as shown below:

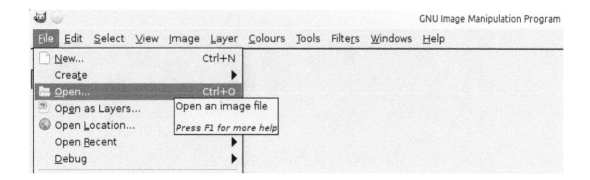

When **Open Image** dialogue box appears, navigate to the file that you want to open (notice the buttons at the top of the window that you can use to navigate to the folders on your computer) and click **Open**:

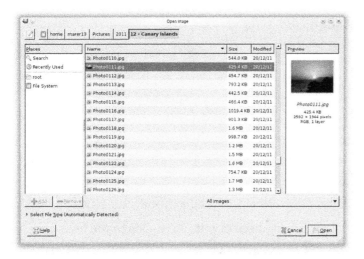

Tool Options panel on the right will display the pixel dimensions of your document so you don't have to look for them (my image is 2592px x 1944px) - screenshot on the next page:

NOTE: If you don't see the Tool Options panel, choose:

Windows > Dockable Dialogues > Tool Options) as shown below:

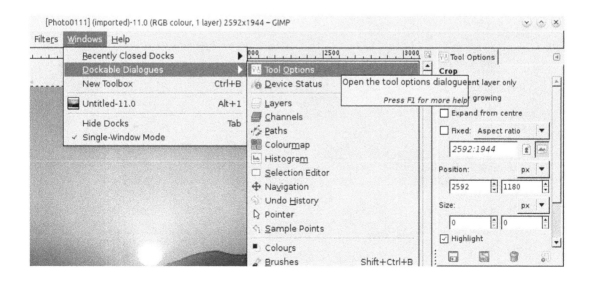

Adjusting the Brightness and Contrast of the image

To adjust the Brightness and Contrast of the image you have a few options. You can use these adjustments:

- *Brightness-Contrast*

- *Levels* or

- *Curves.*

Let's have a look at **Brightness-Contrast** as the easiest.

You will find all these adjustments under the same menu, under Colours. So, with your image open choose Colours > Brightness-Contrast. This opens this dialogue box:

Now, you just start dragging the sliders to adjust the image.

Start with the **Brightness** slider to make the image brighter or darker.

Then move the **Contrast** slider to make the image more or less contrasty.

When happy with the result, click **OK**.

NOTE: If you don't see any changes as you move the sliders, make sure that the **Preview** checkbox is checked in the bottom left corner of the dialogue box. You can also keep clicking on **Preview** checkbox to see before/after effect to compare.

Adjusting the Colours

Let's say you want to adjust the colours in the image. Maybe you want to make colours more saturated or less saturated. A perfect adjustment for adjusting the colours would be either:

- *Colour Balance* or

- *Hue-Saturation*

We'll look at both.

Let's start with **Colour Balance** to adjust the colours within an image.

Open an image that you want to work with and choose **Colours > Colour Balance**:

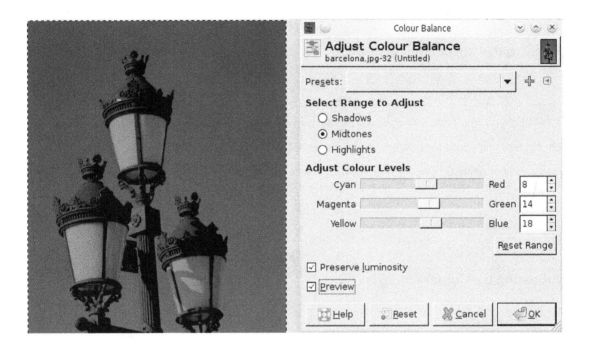

Start moving the sliders under **Adjust Colour Levels**, i.e. if the image is slightly too green, move the Magenta – Green slider to the left to remove the green tint.

When happy with the effect, click **OK** to exit the dialogue box.

Now, you're going to adjust the saturation of the colours in the image with the **Hue-Saturation** adjustment.

With the image opened, choose **Colours > Hue-Saturation**.

Here are two examples with the Saturation moved to right to increase the saturation:

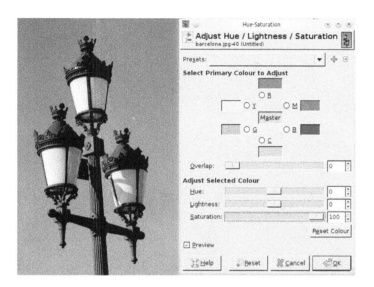

and the Saturation slider moved to the left to decrease the saturation (almost black & white):

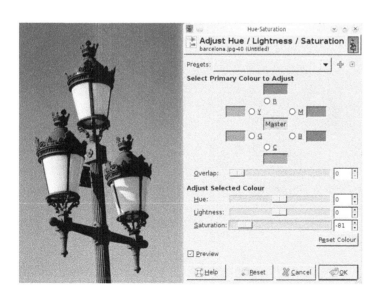

When you're ready to save the image, in Gimp you'll need to export it to save it as either a JPEG, or PNG, or GIF.

Saving Files

To save the file choose **File** > **Export**:

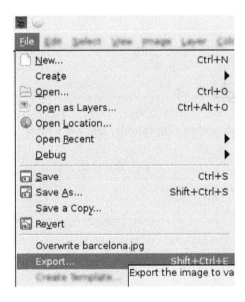

In the Export dialogue box give the file a name as shown on the screenshot on the next page:

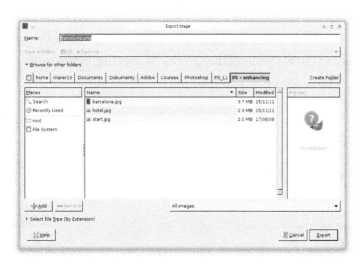

To choose the file format, click on **Select File Type (By Extension)** at the bottom of the screen to reveal the drop-down menu with all the supported file formats. If you don't choose anything here, Gimp will save the file with the same file format as the original, so in most cases you don't need to choose anything here.

Click **Export**.

If you're saving an image as a JPEG, you will now see the **Export image as JPEG** dialogue box like the one below:

Because JPEG is a highly-compressed file format, you use the **Quality** slider to define the compression (the lower the Quality setting the smaller the file size, but also the lower the quality). If you're not concerned about the file size, set the Quality to anything between 90 and 100 (if you're going to print the image, set the Quality to 100).

Click **Export**. Done.

Convert an Image to Black and White

Let's now convert an image to black and white. There is no Black and White adjustment in Gimp, if you looked under Colours menu already. The adjustment you are going to use is **Colours > Desaturate**.

With image opened, choose **Colours > Desaturate**. This opens a dialogue box shown here:

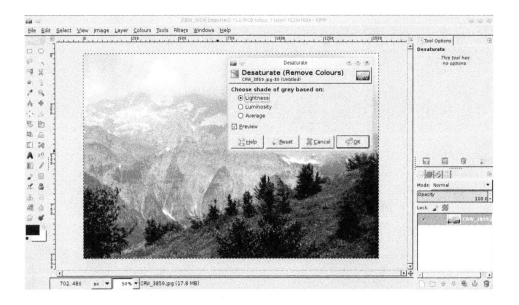

What I can suggest here is for you to try clicking on the options under **Choose shade of grey based on:** and see which effect looks best for you. They all create different black and white effects. Just experiment. Have fun!

When done, click **OK**. Your image is now black and white. Well done!

Save it using **File > Export**.

Working with Layers in Gimp

Gimp, like other graphics editors, supports layers. If you haven't used layers before, they're like transparent sheets stacked one on top of another. Different images or elements can be placed on different layers, which makes them easier to edit. There is no limit to the number of layers you can have in Gimp, the only limit is the amount of memory as each layer uses your memory.

Let's start by looking at the effect you're going to create:

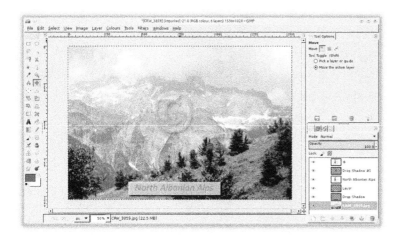

Notice that there are six layers in the Layers panel in the bottom right corner of the Gimp interface:

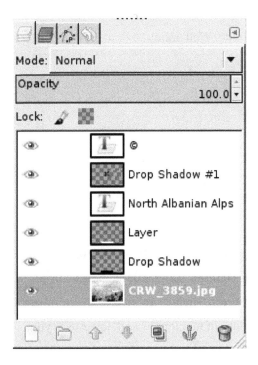

Here's the breakdown of the design and layers structure:

- the bottom layer is the image

- two layers above are the rectangle that appears behind the text (Layer layer) and the drop shadow for the rectangle (Drop Shadow layer)

- above there is a layer with the text (North Albanian Alps layer)

- finally, at the top, there are two layers: copyright layer and shadow layer below (shadow for the copyright symbol.

So, let's get to work.

Start by opening an image that you want to use. That's what your Layers panel should look like, just one layer so far:

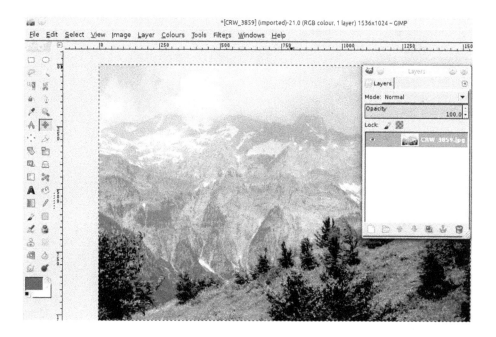

Next, you're going to add a rectangle that will appear behind the main text.

Create a new layer in the Layers panel by clicking on the **New Layer** icon (the icon in the bottom left corner):

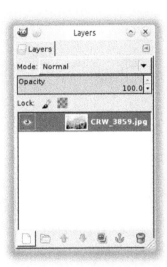

Give it a name, call it **Rectangle** as an example, and leave Layer Fill Type set to:
Transparency. Click **OK**.

You have created a new blank layer.

Now go to the Tools panel and select the **Rectangle Select Tool**:

With the Rectangle Select Tool selected click and drag on the image to create a rectangle.

Next, choose **Edit > Fill with BG Colour**:

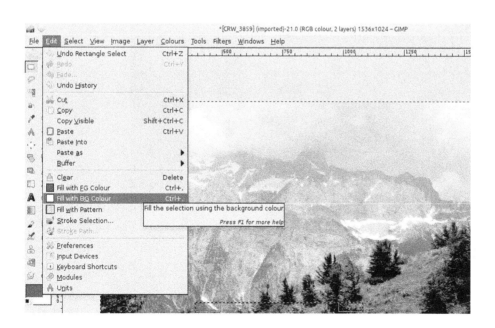

NOTE: BG stands for Background. Your background colour should be white.
If it's not, click on the colour swatch at the bottom of the Tools panel
(the one in the background – that's your background colour)

When you click on it, it opens Change Background Colour dialogue box
in which you can change the background colour by clicking inside
the box on the left in the white area and then clicking OK.

Once you've chosen Fill with BG Colour, the rectangle should have white
fill like the one below:

Now it's time for a shadow. When adding a drop shadow in Gimp, you don't need to create a
new layer, Gimp will create it for you.

Just choose **Filters > Light and Shadow > Drop Shadow...**

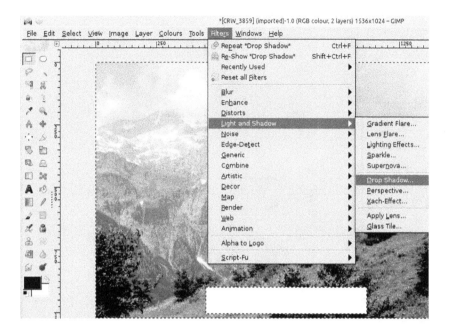

In the Drop Shadow dialogue box accept all the defaults and just click OK.

Congratulations! You have a white rectangle with a drop shadow behind it! Well done!

Now, you're going to make the rectangle semi-transparent, so it shows through the background behind. You're going to do it by reducing the opacity of the layer. The Opacity of the layer defines how opaque or how transparent the layer is.

141

The Opacity slider appears near the top of the Layers panel:

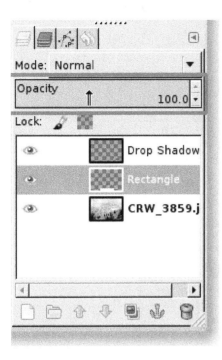

With the Rectangle layer selected, click and drag in the **Opacity** area to drop down the opacity to around **50%** so that the rectangle is semi-transparent and you can see the background behind it.

Click on the top layer (**Drop Shadow layer**) to select it. You're going to add some text now.

When adding text, Gimp creates a new layer for you so you don't have to.

With the top layer selected, select the Text Tool in the Tools panel:

Next, in the **Tool Options** panel set the options for your text:

- *Font Family, Font Size, Colour* etc.

When done, click inside the rectangle on the image and start typing:

If you need to change the colour or size of the text, highlight it and the options box will appear next to it as shown here:

Make changes and then to see how the text updates click on **Move Tool** to deselect the text.

If you have selected the **Move Tool**, you can now move the text to centre it inside the rectangle. Before you click and drag to move the text, check the Tool Options panel. It should be set to: **Move the active layer**:

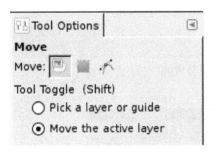

Now you can click and drag to move the text layer.

Next step will be to add a copyright symbol as a watermark to protect your image if you're going to upload it online.

First, find the copyright symbol anywhere and copy it into the clipboard. You can use any document that has a copyright symbol.

Then, in Gimp select the **Text Tool** and click once on a page.

Next, paste the copyright symbol by choosing **Edit > Paste** or by pressing **Ctrl+V**.

Make it big and white in colour (I used 400px Georgia):

North Albanian Alps

Now simply lower the opacity of the layer to around **25-35%** depending on the image. It shouldn't be too distracting.

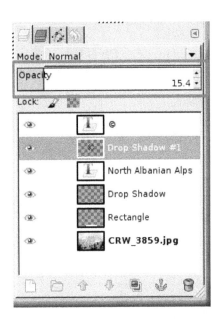

NOTE: If you want to delete a layer, select it and drag it onto a bin icon in the bottom right corner of the layers panel.

Congratulations! You have successfully created a multi-layer document in Gimp. Remember, if you want to email it to someone, export it as a Jpg or Png file using **File > Export**.

Making Selections

Selections are created so that you could work with some areas of the image. Usually we create a selection to move a part of the image onto a new layer or to remove it from the image or blur it as an example.

There are two ways of accessing Selection Tools in Gimp:

from the menu:

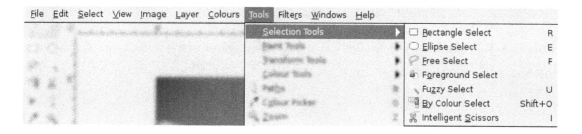

or in the Tools panel:

147

Here's a quick overview of how these tools work:

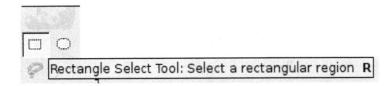

Rectangle Select Tool – it selects rectangular regions of the active layer. It is a very basic tool, but quite often used.

Ellipse Select Tool – it selects elliptical and circular regions of the active layer. Also a basic tool and quite often used.

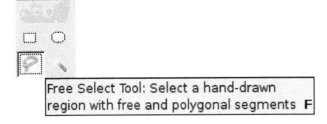

Free Select Tool – a lasso – it creates freehand selections. The selected area closes when you release the mouse button. Good tool if you have a very steady hand, it gives you control over your selection.

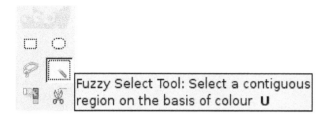

Fuzzy Select Tool – magic wand – it selects the areas of similar colour. When you click on the image with the Fuzzy Select Tool it samples the colour under your cursor and selects all pixels with similar colour within the image.

NOTE: **Fuzzy Select Tool** only selects areas that are adjacent (contiguous regions) unlike the next tool.

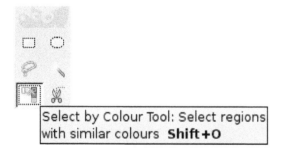

Select by Colour Tool – similar to Fuzzy Select Tool, but it selects all areas of similar colour, even if they're not adjacent (regardless of where they are located).

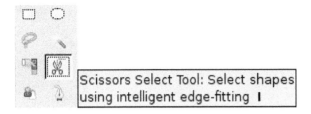

Scissors Select Tool – it is very similar to Magic Wand Tool in Photoshop – it creates anchor points as you click and it tries to detect contrasty edges.

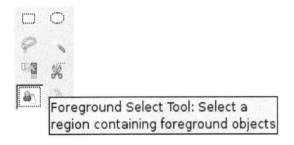

Foreground Select Tool – it lets you extract the foreground from the layer.

And finally:

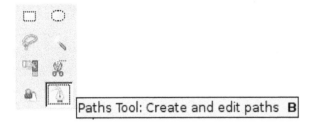

Paths Tool – it is used to create complex selections using Bezier Curves. Anchor points created with the Paths Tool can be edited. Curves created with this tool can be saved or even exported.

Here you go. This is the overview of the selection tools in Gimp.

Managing Photos with Digikam

Digikam is an image organiser and image editor on KDE platform. It supports all major image file formats.

Among its many fantastic features here are just a few:

- *adding captions and ratings*

- *searching through images and saving searches*

- *GPS locator*

- *face detection*

- *exporting images to Flickr, Facebook, Google Earth's KML files, SmugMug etc*

- *burning images on CD*

- *creating Web Galleries*

- *downloading images from cameras/memory cards*

The latest version of Digikam at the time of writing (December 2011) is Digikam 1.9.0:

Digikam doesn't come pre-installed with Kubuntu, so you will need to install it.

1 Open **KpackageKit** and search for **Digikam**:

2 Click on **Install** button and **Apply**. Once Digikam is installed, launch it.

3 When you start **Digikam** for the first time,you need to configure it (as most other applications). Just click **Next**:

4 In the next dialogue box you'll need to point Digikam to a folder where you want to store the images (be default it will use your Pictures folder and that's what I use):

You will also be informed that Digikam stores all the information and metadata about images in a database file which will also be stored in your Pictures folder by default, however you can change that if you want.

NOTE: I would advice to keep images and Digikam database file in the same folder so they're easier to find

5 Next, decide how you want to open raw images (if you shoot raw):

NOTE: **Raw** is a raw file format, equivalent to a digital negative. Many cameras can save files in raw format – all D-SLR cameras and a few digital compacts, other cameras and mobile devices save files in Jpeg format, which is a lossy file format. **Raw** is **lossless**, which means if you shoot raw, you don't loose any data, any quality in your images.

After deciding on how you want to work with raw, click Next.

6 Now, you need to decide if you want to store the information about the files in the files' metadata:

- if you're going to use the images on other photo management applications, click
Add information to files;

- otherwise, if you're only going to use Digikam for all photo management, click
Do nothing:

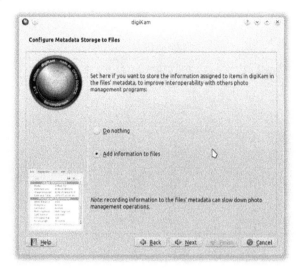

Click **Next**.

7 Now, decide whether you want to display images in preview mode in reduced version or in full version (if you have a slow computer – choose **Load reduced version of image**, on a fast computer – choose **Load image**):

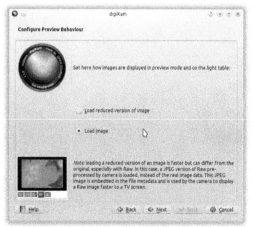

Click **Next**.

8 In the next step, choose what you want to happen when you right-click on the image. You can leave it on a default:

9 Click **Next** to go to the next screen about **Contextual Tooltips**. Choose whether you want to see the Contextual Tooltips and click **Next**.

10 Finally click **Finish**. You're done! Now Digikam will open and will start scanning the folder with your image as shown here:

11 When done scanning, Digikam opens with your library. Here's an overview of Digikam:

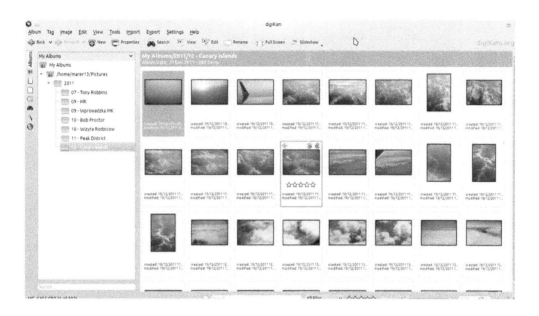

Menu at the top of the application:

Photo albums on the left:

Images within an album on the right:

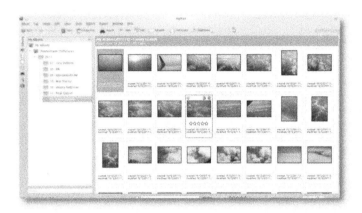

Digikam allows downloading images from digital cameras. To do that, choose **Import >
Cameras**. If Digikam recognises your camera, like in here it recognised my Canon camera,
choose the name that appears on the list:

This will open the **Import** dialogue box where you can preview the images before you import
them:

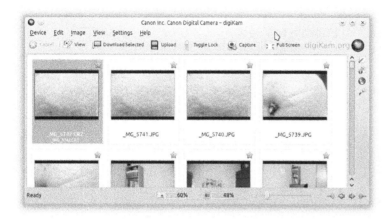

If you look at the bottom of the import dialogue box, you will notice something amazing about Digikam – it displays **available space on the memory card**(!) and **available space in your Library**(!).

Select the images you want to download by clicking on them and click **Download Selected**.

Select Album dialogue box will appear. Choose where you want images to be downloaded and click **OK**.

The download will start, you will see a progress bar at the bottom of the dialogue box and when it's done, it will read **Ready** in the bottom left corner.

Now when you navigate to Digikam you will see the new images! As simple as that!

Congratulations! You have downloaded images from the camera into Digikam. Well done.

Export Images from Digikam

Do you want to export images from Digikam to **Facebook**, **Flickr**, **iPod**, etc.? That's easy. Here's how it's done:

In Digikam, select the images you want to export.

Go to the menu and choose **Export** command:

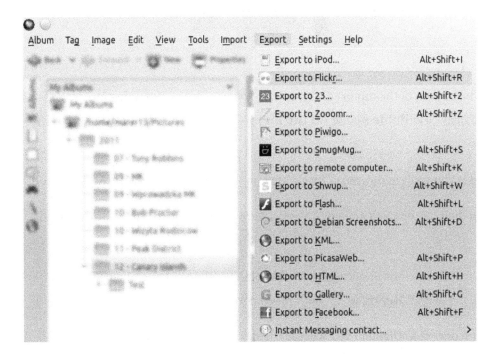

Notice vast number of options available here! You can export your images to almost any online service you can imagine!

Creating Screenshots with KSnapshot

There are several ways to take screenshots in Linux. We all use
our favourite ways of doing it. If you are a Windows user, you have
probably used the Print Screen button on your keyboard and then used one of the graphics
editors to paste it. In Linux we use applications to take screenshots.

Because we're using Kubuntu Linux in this book and it comes with KDE environment, we're
going to use **KSnapshot** – an application that is a part of KDE. **KSnapshot** is one of the
best screen capture applications on Linux and it is very easy to use as well.

Start by launching KSnapshot, you'll find it under **Start > Applications > Graphics**:

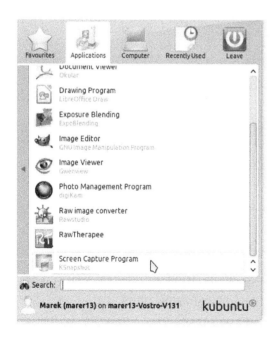

When KSnapshot opens, you have a number of options available under the **Capture Mode** drop-down menu:

Full Screen

Window Under Cursor

Rectangular Region

Freehand Region

Section of Window

You can also include mouse pointer and window decorations (window frame) as well as delay the snapshot by a number of seconds (I use that quite often for Window Under Cursor screenshots).

Once you take a screenshot, you can save it using **Save As...** button in the bottom right corner of the application window.

NOTE: Screenshots can be saved in many file formats, PNG is the best for saving screenshots.

Another interesting option in KSnapshot is the ability to send the screenshot to an external application or online service using the **Send To...** button at the bottom of the application window:

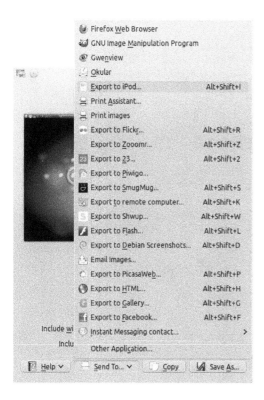

8 Multimedia

It's the twenty first century and more and more people embrace new technologies. With so many people listening to music and watching videos, you may have gathered hundreds of megabytes or more of music and video. You will be happy to hear that the support for playing multimedia on Linux is improving all the time.

Kubuntu/Ubuntu supports many sound cards so yours should be supported and may have been properly detected during installation (I never had any problems with sound cards on the laptops I owned in the past).

To give you a quick overview, there are two main sound card driver' models on the market:

OSS – Open Sound System – with free and commercial drivers;

ALSA – Advanced Linux Sound Architecture – entirely open-source.

Kubuntu uses ALSA and ALSA supports lots of sound cards. If your sound card is not supported, it may be supported in the commercial OSS version.

Linux has a variety of multimedia players for sound and video. We'll focus on the most popular and the easiest to use players.

Sound Volume

For adjusting volume, Linux offers a handy volume slider in the taskbar:

To change the volume, just click on the speaker icon and drag the slider up or down:

NOTE: On some laptops you can also use the volume buttons on the keyboard, it worked on all Dell laptops I have had so far.

Playing Music

Linux has a variety of music players, but the default is **Amarok**.
Amarok is a powerful music player and music management
application. It makes playing music so much more enjoyable than
other music players... and you can see the lyrics as you are listening to your favourite tracks!
(internet connection required).

You can use Amarok to buy and download music and podcasts as well as listen to internet
radio stations and music from USB devices.

When you start Amarok for the first time (you'll find it under **Start > Applications >
Multimedia**), it will scan your home directory for any supported music files and after a
moment it will launch.

Here's the Amarok interface:

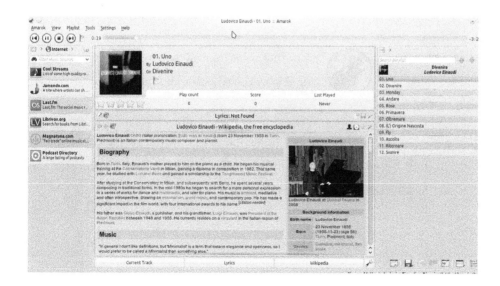

To play music in Amarok:

- choose **Amarok > Play Media...** or

- use the File Manager to find files you want to play, then select them, right-click and choose
Actions > Amarok > Append & Play :

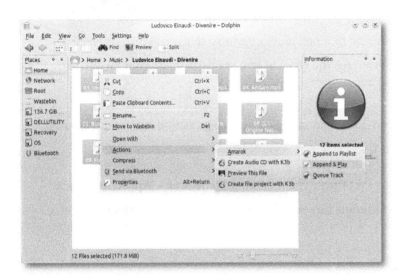

As simple as that. When connected to the Internet, Amarok will display information about the track you're listening to as well as it will display the cd cover and information about the author/album from Wikipedia. Very impressive.

If you're an "old school" music lover that has a collection of CDs (most people nowadays buy music online), then you'll need to install RhythmBox – an application that works well with audio CDs. You can install it straight from KpackageKit.

Watching Videos

Linux recognises many video formats. You may have heard about codecs – encoders and decoders of video. Most of them are proprietary, but there are some free codecs as well.

The most popular video formats are:

.avi – Microsoft format

.wmv – another Microsoft format

.mov – QuickTime format (Apple)

.mpeg – MPEG format

and recently a very popular:

.mkv – Matroska, an open-source, open-standard multimedia container becoming very popular for videos as it supports HD video

Due to licensing restrictions Linux doesn't support natively any proprietary video codecs. However, if you installed third-party software during Linux installation, you will be able to play many video formats. Also, when you install one of the video players, like Mplayer, you will be able to easily play many video file formats.

MPlayer is a very interesting video player that I have used for a number of years.

It supports a wide selection of file formats.

Here's the information from MPlayer's website:

> *It plays most MPEG/VOB, AVI, Ogg/OGM, VIVO, ASF/WMA/*
> *WMV, QT/MOV/MP4, RealMedia, Matroska, NUT, NuppelVideo, FLI, YUV4MPEG,*
> *FILM, RoQ, PVA files, supported by many native, XAnim, and Win32 DLL codecs.*
> *You can watch VideoCD, SVCD, DVD, 3ivx, DivX 3/4/5, WMV and even H.264*
> *movies.*

So **MPlayer** will easily play all sorts of video files.

Here's a screenshot of MPlayer playing an .mov video from a digital SLR camera:

To install MPlayer, use KPackageKit, type **mplayer**, and follow the steps to install it:

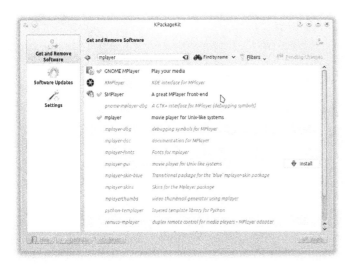

If you're not happy with MPlayer or want to try another video player, another very popular video player on Linux is VLC.

171

Burning CDs and DVDs (BluRay)

In just a moment you are going to find out how easy it is to burn CDs/DVDs/BluRay with Linux! It has never been easier, I find it so much easier on Linux than on other operating systems.

If you have looked through some books on Linux, you may have found it frustrating that many books talk about burning discs using command line. What's funny about that?

It is usually easier to use one of the graphical programmes to burn discs, so that's what I'm going to focus on here. Most computer users don't want to jump into command line (most of you probably don't even know what I'm talking about. Command line...? What's that?). I will talk a bit about command line in Linux near the end of the book. For now, let's just focus on graphical applications.

My favourite, and one that comes with KDE, is **K3b**. I have used **K3b** for a number of years and it still amazes me at what it can do.

If you are a Windows user, you usually need to spend around £50-60 on a software that does what K3b does for FREE! How great is that?

Here's an overview of what K3b can do:

- create Audio CDs

- create Data CDs

- create Video CDs (VCDs, SVCDs)

- CD copy

- CD/DVD ripping

- DVD/BluRay burning

and more.

1 Start by inserting a blank disc into your CD/DVD drive. The following dialogue box will appear:

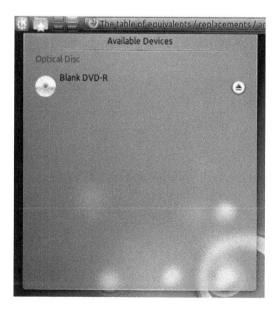

2 Click on the disc icon to open **K3b** (alternatively you can start K3b from the menu, **Start > Applications > Multimedia > Disc Burning**).

Here's the K3b interface when it opens:

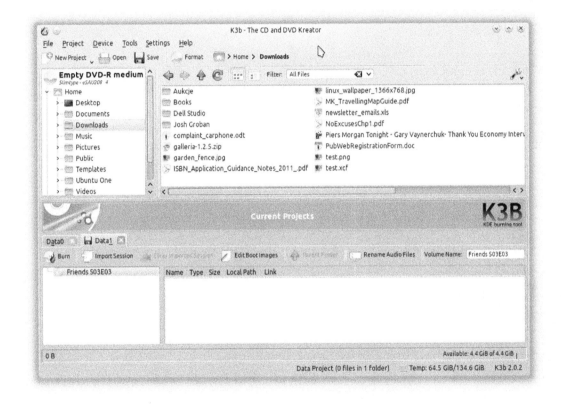

3 In the top part of the application you can navigate through your file system to find files to burn.

4 Files can be added by drag-and-drop to the bottom section of the application window or by double-clicking on the files:

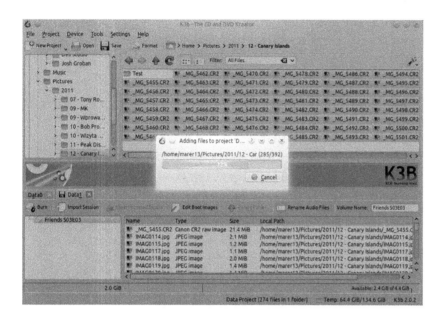

At the bottom of the application window you can see how much space the files will take on the disc (I'm burning a DVD here and files are taking 2.0GB already).

5 To burn the disc, click on **Burn** in the bottom left corner of the application:

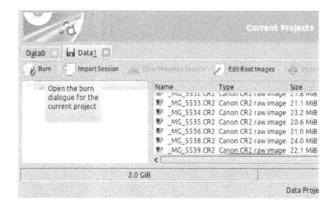

6 This will open burn dialogue box where you can choose how many copies do you want to burn etc. Usually you just leave it as it is and click **Burn**:

7 Alternatively, if you want to give your disk a title, click on **Filesystem** tab and type a name for your disk:

8 When ready to burn the disk, click **Burn** button.

9 This will open **Writing Data Project** dialogue box where you can track the progress:

NOTE: Notice how K3b displays a progress bar in the top left corner of your screen as the project is being burned. Very cool feature!

When K3b finishes burning the disk, the disk will be ejected automatically and you will see a Success message appear as on the screenshot on the next page:

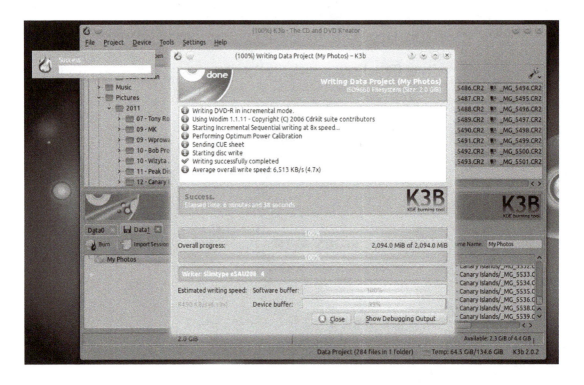

Just click **Close** to exit.

What if you want to burn a different project?

Close the tab for the project/projects in the bottom left corner (mine are named Data0 and Data1) and the screen with different options will appear:

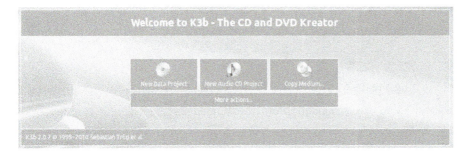

More actions button gives you access to more options:

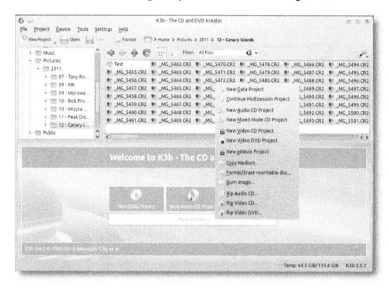

And that's how you use K3b to burn disks.

I encourage you to explore what K3b has to offer.

9 Beyond Basics

Downloading and Installing applications

Installing software in Kubuntu became easy, and many applications
are already installed on your computer when you install Kubuntu
(this also applies to many other Linux distributions nowadays).

However, sometimes you may want to install an application that cannot be installed from
within Kubuntu (or other Linux distribution).

In this case, you would search for it online (like you do when you're looking for an application
for Windows), then download it and install it.

Depending on the application, the authors may only provide downloads for the most popular
Linux distributions (usually Ubuntu/Kubuntu, openSuSe, SuSe, Fedora, Mandriva).

Here's an example from VirtualBox website:

Download VirtualBox for Linux Hosts

VirtualBox 4.1.8 for Linux

Note: The package architecture has to match the Linux kernel architecture, that is, if you a appropriate AMD64 package (it does not matter if you have an Intel or an AMD CPU). Mixed in AMD64 kernel with 32-bit packages) are not supported. To install VirtualBox anyway you need to se

Please choose the appropriate package for your Linux distribution:

- Ubuntu 11.10 ("Oneiric Ocelot") ⇨ i386 | ⇨ AMD64
- Ubuntu 11.04 ("Natty Narwhal") ⇨ i386 | ⇨ AMD64
- Ubuntu 10.10 ("Maverick Meerkat") ⇨ i386 | ⇨ AMD64
- Ubuntu 10.04 LTS ("Lucid Lynx") ⇨ i386 | ⇨ AMD64
- Ubuntu 8.04 LTS ("Hardy Heron") ⇨ i386 | ⇨ AMD64
- Debian 6.0 ("Squeeze") ⇨ i386 | ⇨ AMD64
- Debian 5.0 ("Lenny") ⇨ i386 | ⇨ AMD64
- openSUSE 11.4 / 12.1 ⇨ i386 | ⇨ AMD64
- openSUSE 11.3 ⇨ i386 | ⇨ AMD64
- SUSE Linux Enterprise Server 11 (SLES11) ⇨ i386 | ⇨ AMD64
- SUSE Linux Enterprise Server 10 (SLES10) ⇨ i386 | ⇨ AMD64
- Fedora 16 ("Verne") ⇨ i386 | ⇨ AMD64
- Fedora 15 ("Lovelock") ⇨ i386 | ⇨ AMD64
- Fedora 14 ("Laughlin") ⇨ i386 | ⇨ AMD64
- Mandriva 2011.0 ⇨ i386 | ⇨ AMD64
- Mandriva 2010.0 / 2010.1 ⇨ i386 | ⇨ AMD64
- Red Hat Enterprise Linux 6 ("RHEL6") / Oracle Linux 6 ("OL6") ⇨ i386 | ⇨ AMD64
- Red Hat Enterprise Linux 5 ("RHEL5") / Oracle Linux 5 ("OL5") / CentOS 5 ⇨ i386 | ⇨ AMD64
- Red Hat Enterprise Linux 4 ("RHEL4") / Oracle Linux 4 ("OL4") / CentOS 4 ⇨ i386

So, what you do is choose download for the distribution you are using (choose either **i386** for 32-bit systems or **AMD64** for 64-bit systems).

NOTE: Modern computers are 64-bit machines. If you download the wrong version, Linux will not install it so just download the alternate version.

In this case I'm downloading the version for my system – 64bit Ubuntu 11.04:

Download VirtualBox for Linux Hosts

VirtualBox 4.1.8 for Linux

Note: The package architecture has to match the Linux kernel architecture appropriate AMD64 package. It does not matter if you have an Intel or a AMD64 kernel with 32-bit packages are not supported. To install virtualbox.

Please choose the appropriate package for your Linux distribution:

* Ubuntu 11.10 ("Oneiric Ocelot") → i386 | AMD64
* Ubuntu 11.04 ("Natty Narwhal") → i386 | AMD64
* Ubuntu 10.10 ("Maverick Meerkat") → i386 | AMD64
* Ubuntu 10.04 LTS ("Lucid Lynx") → i386 | AMD64
* Ubuntu 8.04 LTS ("Hardy Heron") → i386 | AMD64

In the dialogue box that opens, leave it as **Open with Gdebi Package Installer** and press **OK**:

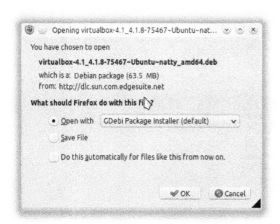

Follow the instructions to install it.

What if you don't want the application you installed and you want to remove it?

That's actually as simple as installing applications.

If you want to remove the application:

1 Open **KpackageKit** and find the application you want to remove.

Now, I may hear you saying "How do I find application I have installed?".

Here's how:

Open **KPackageKit** and click on **Installed Software**:

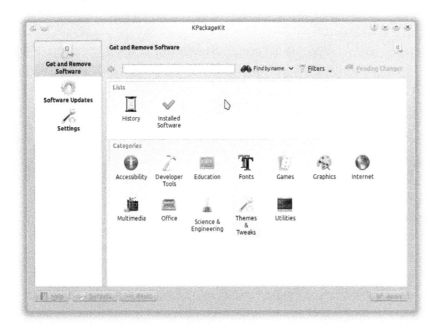

This gives you a list of installed software.

2 Find the application you want to remove and click **Remove** next to it on the right.

Notice that as you highlight the application, description appear at the bottom including the location of the application in the Start menu:

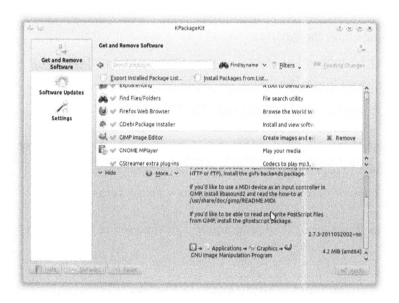

3 So, once you've selected the application to be removed, click **Remove** and **Apply**.

As simple as that!

4 Follow the instructions (type your password) and the application will be removed.

5 When done, close KPackageKit.

NOTE: Unlike in Windows, in Linux you don't have to restart the computer after installing or uninstalling applications.

Using Terminal (Konsole)

If you have been around 'Linux folks' long enough, you may have heard them talk about 'command line' and 'terminal', which sounds a bit like black magic. You would have thought 'Why would I need to use command line? Isn't it a bit too outdated when we live in twenty first century and graphical interfaces do everything for us?' Not really. The command line is one of the most powerful tools in Linux.

Let me tell you something about Linux. At the very heart of Linux operating system is 'kernel' – in simple terms, a programme to communicate with the computer components. A 'shell programme' is a facility that allows Linux users to communicate with the kernel.

Various Linux distributions include several shell programmes. The one you're going to use here will be **Konsole**.

You can open it from the Start menu: **Start > Applications > System > Terminal**.

NOTE: If you cannot find an application, i.e. Konsole, go to Start menu and type konsole in the search box:

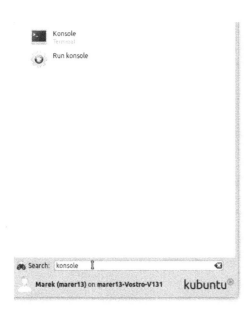

When the application appears, just click on the name to open it.

When Terminal opens, you'll see your username and a blinking cursor:

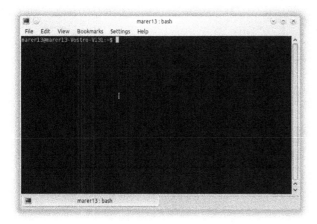

Terminal is now ready to receive a command. Let's get straight to performing some tasks in the Terminal.

Navigate Using Terminal

When you open Terminal, by default you are located in your home directory. Let's see how you can check that.

1 Here's how you can check your current location:

type **pwd**

The **pwd command** displays your current location (in my cases here /home/marer13)

2 To list the content within a folder use **ls** command:

3 To move to another directory, use **cd** command, i.e. **cd Pictures** and then **ls** to display the content with the folder:

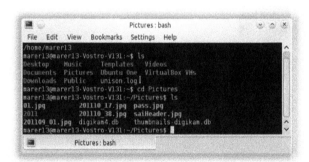

4 To move up the folder hierarchy, use **cd ..** command:

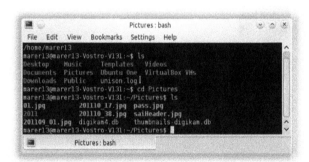

189

5 Now, I'm back to my home directory. I'm going to show you how to go to my Pictures folder and display information about the files within the folder:

Here are the commands:

Here's a breakdown of what I did here:

ls – to list the folder content

cd Pictures – to move to Pictures folder

ls – to list the folder content

cd 2011 – to move to 2011 subfolder

finally, **ls -alt-** to display detailed information about the content within the folder

The list of content is listed by modification time, the latest first, thanks to t in ls -alt command.

Here's what **-alt** in **ls -alt** does:

a – displays all directory contents, including hidden files

l – displays long format listing, including user and group ownership names (in my case marer13 twice)

t – sorts the content by time when files were modified.

Memory Checks

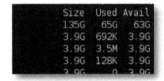

In this section, I'm going to show you how you can perform some memory checks on your system using Terminal (Konsole).

Examine disks and memory available:

Your entire Linux system may work on multiple hard drives and many disk partitions. When you installed Linux, it created some partitions for you automatically. Each partition is represented by a file in the /dev folder, i.e. you can have partitions:

/dev/hda1

/dev/sda1

etc.

To check all the partitions in your Linux system, use df command:

I have here one main hard drive partition - **/dev/sda6** mounted as / (root) with ca.141GB memory and ca.67GB used (51%).

The way the information is presented may put you off and I understand. Let's make it more "user-friendly":

type **df -h**:

-h option makes the output easier to understand, notice that memory is now displayed in Gigabytes instead of bytes.

Now you can see that the actual size of the partition in Gigabytes is 135GB, not 141 as I thought based on bytes values (you may know that 1MB is actually not 1000KB but 1024KB, that's why the difference).

If you want to know what file systems are used on different partitions, add **T** option like that:

df -hT:

Now you can see that the main partition is formatted as **ext4**.

"What if I have Windows running on the same machine or any other operating system and I want to see it here as well?"

Here's what you can do:

1 You will need to become a super-user (like an Administrator) to see that information by typing **sudo** command followed by **fdisk -l**.

2 You will be prompted for a password as a super-user, so just type in a password (you won't see the character) and press Enter. Here's what you're going to see:

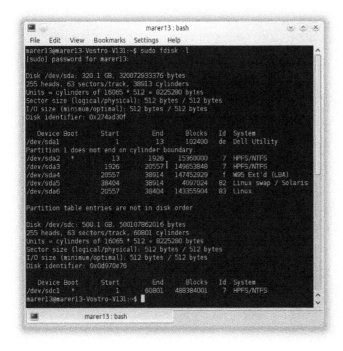

Here's some information about my hard drive:

320GB hard drive mounted as /dev/sda,

Windows partitions in NTFS file system - /dev/sda1, /dev/sda2, /dev/sda3.

Also notice that the external hard drive I have just connected appears here as well:

500GB hard drive mounted as /dev/sdc1 formatted in NTFS.

"What if I want to find out what make my hard drive is and all other details about the hard drive?"

Here's what you can do:

1 Type **sudo dhparm -I /dev/sda** (or other location for hard drive like /dev/sdc1 etc):

My hard drive is a Samsung hard drive – Samsung HM320JI and it is 320GB.

"How can I see how much RAM memory my computer has and how much RAM is being used?"

In the Terminal, type **free -m**:

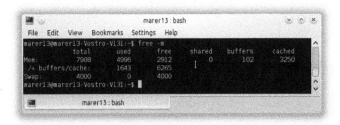

The **-m** option displays memory in MB, in here I have 8GB of RAM (7908MB) and ca.3GB free (2912MB).

"How can I see the processes running at any given time like with Task Manager on Windows?"

Here's what you can do:

Type **ps -e**:

The first line displays the unique **Process ID** (**PID**) and you can use it to shut down a process or application if it doesn't respond with kill command followed by space and PID number, i.e. **kill -38**.

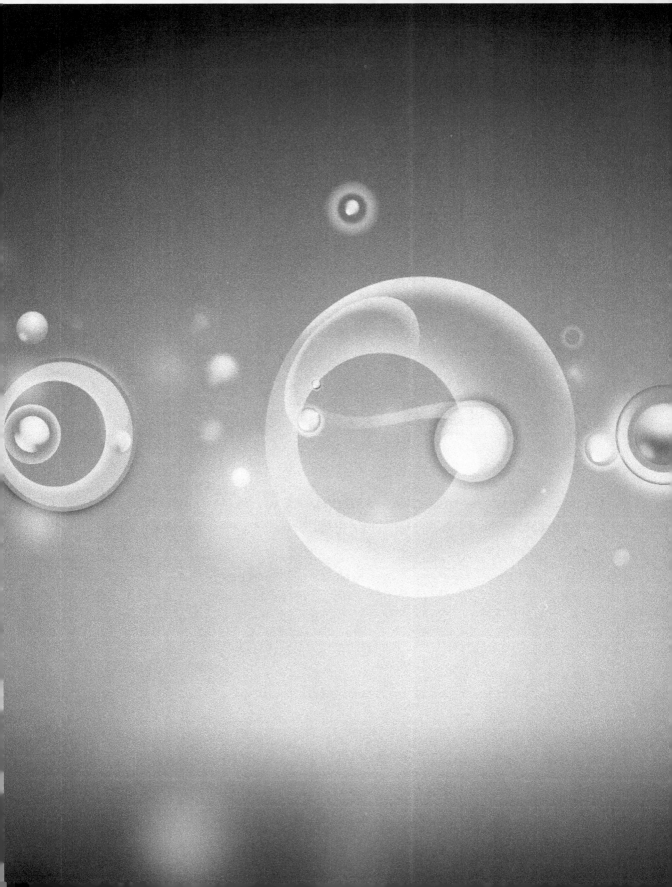

10 Linux equivalents of Windows software

One of the challenges many Windows users have when moving to Linux is finding the applications that will be the Linux equivalents to the applications they use on Windows.

I know this frustration when you move to another operating system and you want to find the applications you want to use and some of them don't exist on another operating system.

Fortunately, many applications (primarily open-source applications) run on many operating systems, so you will find the names of some of the applications on both 'sides' - both operating systems (or in many cases on Windows, Linux, and Mac OS as well).

That's why this chapter is dedicated to doing just that – giving you the Linux equivalents of Windows applications:

A kind of application	Windows	Linux
Internet		
Web browser	Mozilla Firefox	Mozilla Firefox
	Google Chrome	Google Chrome
	Opera	Opera
	Apple Safari	
	Internet Explorer	
		Konqueror
		SeaMonkey
Email client	Mozilla Thunderbird	Mozilla Thunderbird
		Evolution
		KMail
	Outlook Express	

FTP clients	FileZilla	
		Konqueror
		Gftp
		KBear
Instant Messaging Clients	MSN	Kmerlin, aMSN
	Yahoo	Yahoo for UNIX
	AIM	AIM
	Pidgin	Pidgin
		Kopete
Peer-to-peer (P2P) clients	Bittorrent, eMule	KTorrent, eDonkey
	azureus	azureus
VoIP telephony	Skype	Skype
	Buddyphone	Kphone
		Linphone
		Ekiga

Working with Files

Working with compressed files	7-Zip, WinZIP	LinZip, TkZip
	WinRar	
		Ark

Desktop software

Text editors	Notepad	Gedit (Gnome)
	WordPad	Kedit (KDE)
	TextPad	Kate (KDE)
		KWrite (KDE)
		Vim
PDF readers	Adobe Reader	Adobe Reader
		Kpdf
		Okular
		Xpdf
	GhostView	GhostView
		KghostView

Music players	Windows Media Player	
	Winamp	Amarok
		Xine
	SMPlayer	MPlayer
Sound editors	Audacity	Audacity
CD/DVD burning	Nero	Nero
	Roxio Easy Creator	K3b
		XCDRoast
		Gnome Toaster
Video players	Windows Media Player	
	SMPlayer	MPlayer
	RealPlayer	RealPlayer
	VLC	VLC
		Xine
		Dragon Player

Video editing	Adobe Premiere Pro	
		Cinelerra
		CinePaint
		Kino
Bitmap graphics editors	Adobe Photoshop	
	Adobe Fireworks	
	Gimp	Gimp
	Corel Photo Paint	Corel Photo Paint
Vector graphics editors	Adobe Illustrator	
	Corel Draw	Corel Draw
		Inkscape
	LibreOffice Draw	LibreOffice Draw
	OpenOffice Draw	OpenOffice Draw

3D graphics	Maya	Maya
	3D Studio Max	
		Blender
		K3Studio
		K3D
		Moonlight
Office Suite		
	MS Word	LibreOffice Writer
	MS Excel	LibreOffice Calc
	MS PowerPoint	LibreOffice Impress
	MS Access	LibreOffice Base

Index

V

Virtual Desktops 42, 46

W

Watching Videos 169
Weather docklet 104
Web Browser 65
wireless connection 62

www.ingramcontent.com/pod-product-compliance
Lightning Source LLC
Chambersburg PA
CBHW080409060326
40689CB00019B/4181